Oh, To Be A Decorator

JANICE W. HUGHES

Order this book online at www.trafford.com
or email orders@trafford.com

Most Trafford titles are also available at major online book retailers.

Printed in the United States of America.

ISBN: 978-1-4269-4825-1 (sc)
ISBN: 978-1-4269-4824-4 (e)

Trafford rev. 12/10/2010

 www.trafford.com

North America & International
toll-free: 1 888 232 4444 (USA & Canada)
phone: 250 383 6864 ♦ fax: 812 355 4082

Introduction

I have worked in exclusive furniture sales for many years. I have attended many decorator workshops. I am a world traveler. I am also an artist, a poet, a writer, and a decorator.

Decorating is simple if you know what type of furniture to use for your style of home.

Now, eclectic grouping of the three styles of furniture is used as well as antiques. For instance, if your husband insists on using a contemporary sectional, you can use your antique given to you by your aunt if you wish to; it's okay.

If your home is a colonial brick with columns, chances are you prefer traditional furniture mixed with some antiques and early American. Coffee tables made of mahogany wood or maple wood with a rose wood trim and Queen Ann legs are an excellent choice. However, they are very expensive.

We have a flea market sales at First Monday near where we live. All types of furniture are displayed at First Monday every month in Scottsboro, Alabama, at low flea market prices. The sale of the home merchandise is displayed all around the square in nearby Scottsboro, Alabama.

Sometimes used furniture in good condition can set off your room decor and make your room full of furniture look more elegant and exquisite.

It is a good idea to purchase an antique value book. This will enable you to know the value of the purchase you make, whether it is an antique, a dish, or a furniture item.

When purchasing occasional tables for your home, it is more stylish to have three different shapes, such as a round, a square, or an oval or a butler's tray octagonal table.

Oriental rugs are fashionable for a dressy "up town look." They can be used even over a low pile carpet. This gives the room charm and adds warmth.

Wing chairs are necessary for the elegant dressy look.

A ball and claw foot secretary in mahogany would make the room have more atmosphere in a traditional living room; it would add character. Mahogany is a dark wood usually found on most ball and claw secretaries. My grandmother left one to my daughter. The antique adds a lot to the room. It is priceless to her.

If you purchase one on the open market, the cost is usually three to four thousand dollars. Again, if you can find a used one at a flea market, buy it quickly. It is an excellent buy for the living room. If you were fortunate enough to be left any cherry dining room occasional tables or Chippendale chairs in mahogany, cherish them. They make good additions to your home and help give the decor character.

I was asked to help pick out some paint trim for my parents' summer home on the lake soon after I became a decorator. The home had a new roof already installed. The home was of gray rock. The roof was a medium brown. The color was not a good combination. It did not look as though the roof went with the house. Dad had purchased a bargain on the roofing material.

The wooden doors were dressy hand-carved wood in squares. The door pulls were pewter.

I remembered in one of my workshops that a home on the lake or sea front should be a loud, festive color. I could have chosen a turquoise blue. I could have chosen a river green. I could have painted the door a mud color. However, I decided to go with a mauve and paint the doors a slate color because the roof lines were sheik, and the home was in a high-income area. The home was valued at three hundred thousand dollars.

The painters were shocked at the color. However, at my insistence, they began to paint. The mauve brought together the mismatched brown roof and gray rock. It brightened the home up. The doors of slate were lightened up a bit. The door pulls were left a pewter. The home was beautiful and looked what it was worth.

Color is important in the interior of the home as well as on the outside of the home. My many courses in color and trips to many countries helped me in choosing the right color.

You can gage color sometimes by your clothing. For instance, if you wear a navy dress, you might brighten up the color up with red accessories. All that you know comes in handy when it comes to color coordinating. Sometimes three lights and darks of one color bring out the wood, such as dark mauve, medium mauve, and light mauve.

The wood carved door on my dad's lake house could have been in three colors of mauve to show up the woodwork on the door. However, I decided not to do that. The reason was that the house was of a gray rock, and it was cut to look like a long brick.

The roofline was long. The home was contemporary in design. It had a lot of class. The home was sheik.

It had a swimming pool as large as the Holiday Inn's. There was enough wood trim on the house to paint the mauve color, including the private wooden fence that partly surrounded the pool area. The house brought top dollar after a good clean up and a trim paint job of a bright festive color.

After you've decided what colors to use for your home, it's good to draw your rooms off on scale paper before you shop for furniture. First, you need to purchase some scale paper at the store. Each square represents twelve inches. Take a tape measure with you when you go shopping. Also a slide rule is good to have when measuring your floors. The length of the room and the width of the room are what you need. Then draw it off to scale onto the paper. This is much needed so that you can make sure the furniture is spaced far enough apart so you can walk around the room freely with out bumping into it.

Also your furniture needs to be balanced in a room. For instance, if you have a sofa on one side of the room, then perhaps two wing back chairs spaced a little apart for a table and lamp will balance the sofa. This way when some are sitting on the sofa, some guests will sit in the wing chairs. You have to balance the room for good decorating. The chairs don't have to be wing backs; they can be any design you want.

Also the focal point of the room such as a fireplace mantel has to have balance. You need to have the larger piece, such as a mirror, taller in the center and maybe a big vase a little smaller and not as tall by each side of the mirror. Then, if you have room on the hearth, some candles a little shorter on either end of the mantel are nice.

This would be a line elevating up on each side to a point in the center. It is balanced. It's easy to do.

If you have a wall facing the fireplace and have room, you may want to put in a narrow console curio and hang a painting over it. This would balance the opposite side of the fireplace. It's all about walkways, balance, and color.

The fabric you choose as well means a lot. If you want to use the room frequently, you might want to use durable fabric. A sales person is qualified to assist you in this case. Freely ask her, or him, any question about the fabric for your furniture, sofa, and chair purchases.

Accents to a room and accessories are a good mixture to have in your room decor. For instance, a ficus tree set in the corner of the room is all the go now. Also candles set on a cocktail table, the fireplace mantel, and the dining room table are very popular.

If you entertain for a special event such as a wedding, fresh roses or some fresh flowers set in a silver container are called for. However, when you're not entertaining, sometimes silk flowers are a nice arrangement to have.
Aside from silk flowers, real plants of many different kinds of greenery such as ferns and elephant ears scattered throughout the home are a nice touch.

Accessories of many types to accent your decor are in demand for the decorated home. For early American decor, eagles, pilgrims, and baskets of daisies in pictures hung on the walls enhance the early American decor. I saw a painting of a rocker with an afghan folded and placed on the back of the ladder-back rocker. I remember the artist, Hubert Suptrine. I also saw a bucket of apples under a faucet with water running over the bucket and apples. Roosters, ducks, etc., are wonderful complements to the country or early American decor.

Also big poster beds are excellent to use for a country villa or in a farm house with a front porch all the way around the house. Braided rugs are a must for a country look, as are antique headboards, spindle headboards, foot boards, and spindle chairs with early American tables with spindle legs. Spinning wheels, horses, and cows in paintings are also attractive. Just go country all the way when you decorate the farmhouse and the log houses, or if you just simply like the early American country look.

Decorating the old fifty's downstairs level was also interesting. The size of the downstairs made me think of a ship. The living area was paneled with a maple wood. The fireplace was made of old brick. The brick had been taken from an old burned building. The color of the brick was mauve, silver, and slate. There was a maple wood mantel and an opening at the end of the hearth for a small TV. The kitchen was long, and the appliances were built in. There was a place under the stairs for a small refrigerator. Near the sink on the left side was a small opening for a built-in refrigerator. Two Dutch ovens occupied a space in this kitchen. It was neat. The cabinets were maple with indirect lighting over the cabinets.

There was one master bedroom with double closets, a huge window, and a space for a TV on the opposite wall of the bed. Down the hall were three bedrooms, one small bedroom and two a little larger. A linen closet was at the end of the hall.

The whole downstairs was paneled with maple paneling.

I started in the kitchen. I painted the cabinets a maple color. I had new almond appliances installed in their spaces. I had the carpet pulled up in the living space, and I had the wooden floors painted a high gloss of maple color on the floors to look as if it were on a ship. I put down a braided rug and added a plaid sofa with some beige, mauve, and brown colors.

I put two leather chairs and ottomans opposite the sofa in front of the TV and fireplace. I put a board with a small inner tube flat and glued on a small paddle and mounted it on the wall over the sofa. Wooden lamps were put on two small lamp tables beside the sofa. A life preserver was hung on the wall above the fireplace. A large wall clock hung on the opposite wall. I put a round table in a small place in the end of the kitchen. I placed a small candleholder on a tablecloth on the table. On a piece of board, I mounted a bell at the bottom of the stairs along with a ship's steering wheel.

In the large bedroom I had a large headboard made for a wall mount covered in a beige textured fabric to simulate a suite on a ship. Two wall lights were mounted on the wall above two pieces of wood for a nightstand. I used a small dresser and a small mirror mounted on the wall above the small dresser.

In the back room, I had the walls painted in a sky blue with sea gulls flying in the clouds. On the bottom half of the room's walls, I had an artist paint the wall to look like the inside of a ship, complete with life jackets and life preservers, along with small boats painted on. Then I had a whirlpool installed.

The downstairs was complete. It made me feel as though I was on a ship -- the high gloss floors, the round porthole, simulated windows with a sea picture inside the round window frames. It was now not only a downstairs level, but also an escape from one's daily routine.

The upstairs was done in a ritzy New York apartment look. Everyone was pleased with the decor on the two levels.

You can make a name for yourself if you're a designer by simply using the theme decorating idea. Also have your name in small print on a four-inch wooden board mounted somewhere on the bottom part of the room of the homes you have decorated. Also you might ask the homeowners to recommend you to a client if they like your home decor. Word of mouth is the best way to get your name out there.

When you've had decorator training and have worked in decorating many homes, upon entering a room that needs decorating, you can get a mental picture of what the room would look like if you decorated it. For instance, my husband and I went to see his aunt in Arlington, Virginia, the other day.

I went downstairs for something for her and became astonished at the possibilities of the room being decorated as if it were a VP waiting room in an airport. I could imagine the posts having boards with arrows painted on them in different directions, and I envisioned a purple indoor-outdoor carpet on the floor. I could envision small pictures on the windows and on the walls posters of airplanes. There could be added small metal chairs that could probably be purchased from an office supply or a doctor's waiting room that is being moved to another location. I would have wall mounts for small televisions and a wet bar and some stools.

There was also a bathroom down there. I could paint a woman's and a man's outline on the door. I could see some round tables with chairs and some twin-sized beds up against the walls with bolster pillows with some room dividers for privacy.

I saw all this in my mind before going back upstairs at my husband's aunt's. You just do that when you are a decorator. It could be done easily.

Fabrics are important in the durability of your new sofa ensemble. Cotton and polyester blends in a number of prints are widely used on the casual sofas. Polished cotton blends and a velvet look are used for formal living areas: red violet and red, red orange, orange, yellow orange, yellow green, green, blue green, blue violet.

The three secondary colors orange, violet, and green are made by mixing equal parts of two primary colors. At this point, fasten your seat belts because you're headed for a color eruption. By mixing the primary and secondary colors, you will come up with six intermediate or tertiary colors. Tint a hue lighter by adding white; shade it darker by black; dull its intensity by adding gray.

There are several ways to build a color scheme by playing with the color wheel. A monochromatic scheme is based on tints and shades of a single color because their color variation (black, white, and neutrals don't count) texture becomes important in order to avoid monotony.

Like a plaid joined with chairs of a textured fabric, an analogous color scheme makes use of colors used side by side on the color wheel. You'll use these base-related, like yellow, yellow-green, and green, interesting because of the change of pace and value, of color.

A complimentary scheme is based on using colors that are opposite the color wheel, like blue and orange, or red and green. They create a sharp, decisive look, particularly suitable for contemporary rooms. Be sure that one color leads, with the others as accents.

I enjoy taking my colors from the fabric I choose. I simply admire the fabric and its color and design. The design of the fabric you choose, whether it be a colorful design or a plaid or a multi-color fabric. Take your color scheme from these fabrics. A bold orange and navy and hunter green fabric for your sofa in a den maybe with a coordinating plaid large reclines with a multi-color fabric with some of the same coordinating colors in another comfortable chair with an early American style sofa or a traditional one is good decorating. This room will show off your color scheme.

If the outside of your home is a smooth line contemporary design, then chances are you prefer contemporary design furniture. Think pieces all the way –– cubes, circles, and squares. These are the shapes of the cocktail and accessory tables to be used.

Glass square tables with plain square sectionals are usually called for in the contemporary decor. In the bedroom a contemporary wall bed with a lighted headboard is nice. A modern statue in a spacious living area is a pretty accent piece to use. It is a nice conversation piece to add to your contemporary home decor.

I like to think of a high rise apartment when I think contemporary. Just imagine an Oriental white sofa with square accent tables in mahogany mixed with some Oriental Chippendale chairs and an off-white Oriental rug with a pole light for extra soft light and a modern design painting over the sofa or the fireplace.

Do you get the picture? Yes, Oriental Chippendale can be used with contemporary easily. It gives the room an uptown look. Modern glass candlestick holders and pastel candles give the room a romantic warm feeling. This is called putting on the Ritz.

Of course, you don't have to spend a fortune. Cover a square frame sofa with a silk blend white fabric with an imprint design. Use a flea market find of contemporary oak and glass square cocktail table with matching end tables, and there you have it, a swanky uptown look. Bring out the candles; purchase a flea market find of plain candleholders, and the room will look as though you spent a small fortune.

It's the room as a whole that comes together that makes a professional look. Comments on a room well done should be "I love the room." "Everything in this room is well coordinated." "I just don't know what piece of furniture it is that makes this room look great."

In other words, try not to have a single piece of furniture stand out. Try not to have a star piece unless you have a magnificent piece you want as your focal point.

If you have a fancy mirror that overpowers the fireplace mantel and that is a magnificent antique, then go ahead and do it. The company you invited will talk about it. Their eye will go directly to the oversized mirror. And, you will have successfully shown off the prize piece.

Pink light bulbs can be purchased to give the room a more complimentary lighting effect. Decorators often suggest pink lighting.

Although lace curtains were used in the eighteenth century for draperies, they are still good today. The curtain rod should be hung eight inches above the curtain window. A three-inch width hem allowance should be on each side of the curtain. Also an eight-inch hem allowance is correct at the hem of your curtain.

My parents always had a decorator make their curtains. I noticed how well they were made as a child. There were even small weights at the edge and center of their curtains. This was to hold the curtain in the correct place and keep the hemline down where it belonged.

Today, window treatments are widely used. A curtain valance with a blind is widely used. However, I prefer a curtain rod that accents the type of period furniture I use.

For instance, when using a mixture of Queen Anne and traditional and French together, a wooden fancy curtain rod is good to use. Polished cotton with a flat rod of sheers of white and tie backs are flattering to use in such a décor, and so are lace curtains. A curtain is needed when you want privacy. If your home is far off the highway and no one can see in your windows, try not using curtains. The sunlight and the feeling of being out in nature are good to have in your home atmosphere.

Wooden curtain valances are out of date. However, some decorators use them in children's rooms all the way across for special decorating, such as displaying a nursery rhyme like "Peter Cottontail." It could be written onto the wooden curtain valance.

In special rooms the decorator uses whatever is called for. In a stately room of a silk blend material, a cloth valance is better than a wooden one. I prefer just a plain curtain of good material with no valance.

A stately or traditional design of furniture is best for the colonial brick home with columns. It is a combination of Queen Anne, Hepple white, and French in design.

You may find this combination in most all home magazines. The White House and all heads of state such as governors use this combination of design of furniture. It is also widely used by the wealthy. Rose wood, mahogany wood, cherry wood, and maple wood are mostly used in the stately design furniture. They are your best hard woods.

The movie *Father of the Bride* and the TV sitcom with Michael J. Fox as a senator display the stately furniture. If you rent the movies *Sleeping with Enemy* and *Father of the Bride,* run back over the movies slowly.

For instance, in *Sleeping with the Enemy,* when the star leaves the enemy, her husband, she leaves a contemporary designed home on the ocean front and goes to a farmhouse with a big front porch -- a complete opposite from the modular design furniture in the contemporary oceanfront home. The farmhouse is completely country in design and is a mixture of antique beds, ruffle skirt chairs, and draperies. The kitchen is country as well.

However, in *Father of the Bride* the traditional design furniture look was used throughout the home. The color scheme was excellent also. The dining room table used was a cherry wood along with Queen Anne chairs. The furniture in *Father of the Bride* was a classic mixture of traditional, Queen Anne, and French.

After viewing these films, you will have a better understanding of what design furniture mixture you most want for your home.

Also Oriental furniture such as black lacquer goes well with any plain line of furniture. Sometimes a dining room of Oriental design is chosen, although the living room is a mixture of furniture. However, it is a good idea to use plain straight lines of furniture when mixing Oriental with your décor -- again, modern mixed with Oriental.

The shutters and colonial home with columns are best for the traditional design furniture and stately mixture.

The old colonial homes are better decorated in a classic way. In other words use authentic accent pieces. You may want to check out of the library a history of George Washington or maybe Louie the 14th and 15th. You could use traditional and early American furniture with Queen Anne accessories and some blends of antiques. You might want to go with strictly early American. An idea for the dining room, purchase an American flag. Either purchase plain white wallpaper and use the flag as a guide line of the stripes to draw on the wall or the wallpaper. The room should look like a flag on the walls of red and white when you get through. However, you may want to use plain off-white walls and navy or red striped balloon curtains or plain red curtains with gold stars on them. A cheery or mahogany dining room suite is nice if you prefer a dark wood early American dining room group.

If the dining room is a dressy one with a cherry or mahogany dining room suite that is in a high varnish, then use fine china and purchase a picture in a dark frame of George and Martha Washington. Old poster beds are called for in the bedrooms and also lace curtains with wooden rods are what they used a century ago. It's authentic decorating. An antique sofa with a rose carved on the back of the sofa is a nice added feature. They have reproductions of these antiques. Look for antique reproductions for your old historical homes. They compliment the period of the home.

The foyer of the home is usually decked with a hall tree and an umbrella stand along with some ferns on a plant stand. Wing chairs are usually put by the fireplace. The kitchens are usually out of date; however, add an island for a workspace. These kitchens are, as a rule, very large. Have indirect lighting put in; put in some stained glass windows for your windows to add atmosphere and privacy.

When you have decorated to perfection and you don't live in the home long, you will create a high selling price for your home and furniture. The home will be marvelously attractive and in the correct decor for the period. You can make some money on the home in the resale market.

Theme decorating is all the go now. You can make a room look any way you want and have any type feel. For instance, if you want a feeling of floating on a cloud in a bedroom, just paint the room light blue, and then paint white clouds all around the walls. Use light, off-white carpet. A Hollywood bed frame in king size is widely used for comfort. You will have the feeling of floating on a cloud. It's a calm feeling, and the stress of the day will disappear. You will most probably sleep well.

If you like the outside and camping, how do you like the idea of a waterfall mural in your bedroom? Put the mural up on the bedroom walls. Use grass green or gray rock color carpet and slide a queen-sized bed frame up against the water fall mural. Use a green and light brown and amber leaf print spread and drapes. You will feel as though you're outside. You will feel serene if you love camping. If you want to, you can even paint tiny, silver stars on the ceiling of your bedroom.

Go ahead and try your fantasy. It's your home and your dream of what is a good feeling for you.

My husband and I decided to purchase a hot tub. We had a room downstairs we did not use. It had no windows. I decided to put up some wallpaper to make it feel as though we were in the jungle. I got the idea when we were in Hawaii. There was jungle wallpaper in the hotel where we stayed.

I told the lady at the wallpaper store about the wallpaper. She checked into it, and I ordered the wallpaper. I had the wallpaper put on the walls. I purchased a large hot tub and had it installed in the room. I also purchased a tape of the sounds of nature in the jungle at the store. We feel so relaxed when we use our hot tub. We sleep well after sitting in our jungle hot tub in our room.

If your home is a French Tudor design, then the fireplace should display an iron pot and a pot holder. An early American dark pine open China table with hutch is probably your best choice for the dining area. However, you might be able to find an old antique mahogany Jacobean table and chairs. An early American oak wash table is also correct, as well as a spindle back chairs. Shaker furniture is good to use as well. However, I prefer the big early American look or the Jacobean furniture.

In the living room, country French or early American furniture is called for. A hickory chair makes an excellent coup-French group complete with wide French chairs with a cotton blend fabric with a ruffle at the bottom of the chairs and sofas. Big poster beds are in order for the many bedrooms. Rice carved beds and armoires are good to use in the large bedrooms. These homes have a lot of atmosphere. They make you think of being in the English countryside. These homes are best placed on several-acre areas of land.

In a log home, simple, simple is the decor. You may use old wooden tables. I have an idea. Say you found an old farm house Shaker table at the flea market. Just take a chain and swing it over your left arm and let it fall easily over the old table, hitting the table lightly from end to end, three inches apart until you have covered the entire table. It is not necessary to do the legs of the table; they might be damaged in the process. However, if you feel you must have the distressed look on the table, hold the chair in your hand about one inch from the leg. Lightly tap the leg all over for a distressed look, but remember to be careful not to damage the furniture piece.

After you have completed the "destressing" of the old table, go to the art shop and purchase some antiquing kits, or paint the table a Williamsburg blue: a blue gray.

Braided rugs are called for. Kerosene lamps are a nice light for the homes. Homemade quilts are good to use on the beds. Remember, the more rustic the furniture, the better.

Wood groups in pine with cushions are an excellent choice. The fabrics come in a nylon with daisies or an old spinning wheel fabric pattern. I think they're made in Athens, Tennessee. You might find one at a flea market. Country plates and jars for drinking glasses are excellent authentic choices for the old log homes.

Decorating problems in the home can be corrected. For instance, a dining room with no room for much furniture you could add a narrow library table. That might help with the lack of space in the room. Also two small china hutches built in may help. When I was a teen, I remember my mother having a decorator. She decorated a small porch area of the home into a dining room for our summer home, which we sometimes used for a winter retreat.

The decorator, at Mom's request, held down the cost of the decor. She found a narrow Spanish design table with strong black leather Spanish chairs. The decorator had a cabinetmaker build in two cabinets on each end of the room for some dishes and some accessories. The cabinets were all the way to the floor. Wine carpet was used. She painted the cabinets a celery color to blend with the colors in the other part of the house. These were colors opposite the color wheels. However, they blended well.

To carry out the color selection, the decorator used two wine chairs and a Spanish table in the foyer overlooking the pool area. The master bedroom was the next room after entering the foyer. There the walls were again celery in color. The colors blended well with the dining room. Today instead of wine carpet, most probably mane would be the color used.

I had a decorating problem in my kitchen. We had old pine cabinets. John, my husband, wanted to keep the cabinets. I didn't argue with him. I had old cabinets, but they were in good condition. They were painted in a clear varnish to dress them up. I then chose a bright floral wallpaper of blue, orange, and pink. I also purchased wallpaper that had fabric that matched the floral print.

I had a curtain valance of the same fabric put up and added a small tassel trim. The draperies were draw drapes. The tablecloth for the round table was in a plaid of the same colors as the wallpaper.

The place setting was of a China in a coordinating color. The glasses were pink. When I had guests over for a small dinner, they commented on how beautiful the kitchen was. "This is a doll kitchen." "This is the prettiest room in the house." No one ever noticed the out-of-date cabinets.

Decorate a room in your home to give you the feeling you're on an island -- or perhaps a waiting room in an airport. Use the African influence or just use your imagination. For instance, what is your favorite place? After you decide, then decorate accordingly. Make your home an escape from your daily routine, or just make it tastefully decorated and comfortable. You're in command of your own space in your abode.

My daughter and son-in-law just purchased a new home. It is simply beautiful. The ceilings are high, and there are many rooms. Just as you come into the foyer of the home, there are high ceilings and a large wall space to decorate in front of the staircase. The dining room is to the left of the foyer just as you enter the home. The furniture is French and off white in color.

Renoir, pronounced "ren-wah", was a French impressionist artist, one of the old masters. He painted events such as picnics, boat rides, and ladies and gentleman in fancy attire. He caught French girls in ballet, in fancy hats, and in many more dressy events.

I had a brainstorm about decorating the high walls in the foyer of my daughter's home.

She had a beautiful wedding, and all the bridesmaids were young and beautiful. The photographer caught them on film in the room just before the wedding. The dresses were dark peach. The bridesmaids had fancy floral bands in their hair. My daughter had on a beautiful white wedding gown with a lot of beesa with a pearl necklace also.

We decided to have that picture blown up to a very large one; we touched it up to show off the pretty young faces of the bridesmaids and the bride. It was beautiful.

The frame chosen was a gold baroque. Beside the bridesmaids was another space, a very large one. We decided to again blow up another wedding picture. We decided on the punch bowl and a few bridesmaids serving the punch -- also the little basket carrying flower girls.

When you enter the foyer of the home, you see a picture to your left on the upper wall; it is a beautiful picture of the young girls and the bride smiling. It has been touched up by the photographer with paint. You have to look closely to see if it's a Renoir painting.

Also to the left before entering the French dining room is a small picture of the little flower girls in their eventful attire. It also looks as if it might be a Renoir. It is a unique idea for your large wall space.

The next thing to master is the theme in decorating your main home or your summer home. Our home, for instance, is a traditional brick. The front is decorated by an early American curvy wood frame and early American columns. The back of the home has solid glass across the whole back of the house. I could have gone traditional or contemporary; either one would have been correct.

It was time to redo our home. We removed all the old furniture. We also removed the old draperies. In the living room were some velvet draperies. I had a glass chandelier. It was a formal look. I took a good look at the room after the furniture was removed and the velvet draperies. I did not want the room to be very formal again. However, I did want a dressy look.

I stood back in the living room and noticed how beautiful the cathedral ceiling looked. The fireplace had a beautiful hearth, and the whole wall was covered in mountain pastel rock. There was also a mantel made out of the rock. The floor was squares of wood. One side of the room was solid glass sliding doors. A terrace was just outside the window.

After cleaning the room thoroughly, I decided to decorate, picking up the colors from the mountain rock of the focal point -- the fireplace. I purchased a thick-pillowed, light off-white sofa and love settee. The pillows were the colors in the rock: mauve, light blue, and pinkish beige. I decided upon using an Oriental rug in front of the sofa of pastel colors. I chose a small round cocktail table of maple trim wood and a square and oval end table. An antique brass chandelier I chose to hang just below the maple colored cathedral ceiling.

Draperies were not needed since we were so far off the road from the back. However, I chose a polished cotton of light beige to match the rug. A dull brass curtain rod and curtains were chosen to hold the plain draperies for this room. The draperies were only used for when the sun was brightly shining into the room and at night.

Pillows of mauve were used on the hearth for seating for special occasions. The room was dressy without being overpoweringly formal. It was a pleasant experience sitting in the room after the decorating changeover. How to purchase furniture and items for your home:

Be sure all the furniture you purchase fits the room. Don't overpower the room with furniture. You want to be able to walk around the room without bumping into any piece of furniture. Most bedrooms are too small for a king-sized bed. However, if you must have one, leave off the nightstand and hang up two wall lights on either side of your bed for lighting. You might want to leave off a dresser and have two small chests. Just remember to allow for enough space for your furniture.

If you're planning on purchasing a comfortable chair for the den, Recliners are widely chosen and are a good choice.

However, a nice, more dressy chair is the leather chair and ottoman. They're better looking and very comfortable. The in colors and type fabric chosen for the chairs and ottomans is leather; the colors are oxblood (which is a brownish red wine color), navy, blue, and neutral, as in various shades of beige. Almost always decorators prefer a leather chair and ottoman instead of the widely used recliner.

Accents to a room and accessories are a good mixture to have with your room decor. Candles on the coffee table, the fireplace mantel, and the dining room table are also popular. A centerpiece on a table in the dining room is nice to have.

Aside from silk flowers, a real plant of many kinds of greenery is in style throughout the living area and in the foyer. Accessories of many kinds help make the decor complete, for instance, eagles, brass, and pictures of pilgrims and baskets with daisies in paintings.

For instance, I saw a painting of an old rocking chair with an afghan folded over the back. I remember the name of the artist; it was Hubert Subtrine. Prints of the rocker-afghan wouldn't be very expensive to purchase if you like the early American look, sometimes called a country look. Any accessory or painting would work, for instance a painting of wood and daises or a bucket of apples under a faucet. Baskets, pewter, and pictures of an old barn or roosters, ducks, etc. Get the idea of what to use for your accessories if you want a country look?

In one of my many workshop classes, I learned about a technique called a waxed fruit effect on the walls. This technique works well with velvet curtains and silk sofas and chairs. Glass chandeliers would be an excellent choice also with the high gloss walls.

I purchased some aborigine paint and also some medium apricot color interior wall paint. I painted the walls with some of each color paint to see the effect of the colors with the high gloss over it. It was beautiful and elegant, very unique. It did look like waxed fruit. This is a new idea to use when painting sheet rock walls for an elegant look.

I helped in decorating one of my friend's children's rooms. I decided to paint the walls an ocean blue. I painted them a medium blue, turquoise, and dark blue. I drew a large circle on the ceiling with points all around it. I then painted the circle and points orange to represent the sun.

I then painted some different colors of green on the walls for seaweed. Then I painted some fish on the wall of orange, yellow, and gold. I got creative and painted some bubbles coming up from a child swimming with goggles on, on the wall. It appeared as if the child was swimming underwater with the fish. I found a headboard that looked like a seashell. I Painted it gray.

My friend was pleased and her little girl was also. The child liked the water effect. The room had the effect of living under the water. I used dark blue carpet and draperies.

I got the idea when my friend told me her little girl enjoyed Florida and enjoyed swimming. An idea on the sea painted wall room if you leave out the swimming child painted on the wall. You could add a wooden board with

my poem on it.

If I Were A Fish

If I were a fish

I would explore the ocean floor

If I had my druthers

My colors would be orange and black

I'd swim the limpid pools

With the fish of schools

I'd soar to the ocean top

And jump up in midair

And return to the ocean blue as good as new

If I were a fish

I'd swim the ocean's depths

Alongside the mighty whale

There I'd always prevail

Swimming in the ocean pool

If I were a fish

I'd swish and swish and swish

Also on the bed you might want to add some fish pillows, an orange and black fish with some seashell cushions, and maybe a seahorse pillow. You can draw the designs on paper and then use them as patterns. It's an original idea for a child's room. It gives the effect of living in the water.

Table Of Contents

Dedication 29

The Taste Of Cinnamon Years.................................31

Memories 42

The Young Married Years 77

Beginning In Business 90

Decorating Advice...101

Selected Poems 125

Dedication

This book is dedicated to Melody, my granddaughter.

The Taste Of Cinnamon Years

I was born on April 17, 1947. My parents were Jo John Williams and Peggy Raulston Williams. Mother and Daddy were in their early twenties when I was born. Daddy served in the Navy and I was born while he was in the service. I was a baby boomer; being born during the baby boom.

My parents purchased their first home when I was five years old. It was located at the foot of Battery Hill in small Alabama town.

Dad and his brother opened a business supply company. I could see it from our picture window. The home was small at first, but Daddy had a room built overlooking the town. A garage was underneath the long room with windows. Windows were all around the newly built room. Daddy had tile put on the floors. A long table was at one end of the room. A sofa, chair and a television were at the other end. A small kitchen was next to the large, newly built room.

The garage walls gave the room some support, as well as the floor. Daddy also built two bedrooms onto the other end of the house. We enjoyed the home. The house was stucco and Daddy had the hardwood floors refinished. The living room was small and the dining room was directly behind the living room hall. The house consisted of one small bathroom and three bedrooms. We had a large front lawn as well as a back lawn.

Daddy built a block grill to grill on when we had hamburgers and steaks. We all liked charcoal steaks as well as charcoal hamburgers. Mother prepared dishes to go with the meals. She always cut up large tomatoes and purple onions to serve on the hamburgers. Mother liked German chocolate cake. She would prepare it in a long cake pan and then cut it into small squares.

We enjoyed the den as we called it. We ate on the long table in the den. After dinner, we watched television at the end of the long room. Daddy had a TV mounted in the corner of the huge room.

Janice, Peggy, Rudder, and Daddy, sitting on a sofa.

I got a baton for Christmas one year. The next-door neighbors were the Smiths. Their daughter Judy was a majorette. I watched her twirl her baton in her backyard. She waved and invited me over to watch her. She taught me the basics of baton twirling -- the two-hand spin, the vertical twirl, and how to hold the baton. She then showed me her baton collection. Judy had a blue sparkly baton. I was awed by her collection and her uniform.

Granny, Daddy's mother Ruby Parton, was impressed with my twirling and, of course, "how cute" I was, as she said. I had blue eyes and naturally curly blonde hair. I called her "Granny." She took me over to see the band director, Mr. Jones. He smiled as we entered the band room. Granny was a respectable citizen of the small town. Mr. Jones knew her through Papa's business. He owned an appliance store in the downtown area. Mr. Jones had done some business with him when he and his family moved to town. Granny answered the phone for Papa a few days a week. Granny and Mr. Jones had met at the store.

Granny told him that Judy had mentioned they were interested in adding a mascot to the majorette squad. Mr. Jones said that he would be delighted to do just that. Granny was pleased and we left the band room happy.

I could taste cinnamon as the fitter at Button and Badge fitted me in my new satin uniform. I also got some white boots. I remember the leather smell of the boots. A white hat topped off the outfit. I remember marching in front of the band with the majorette squad downtown one Thanksgiving.

Mom always had a pan of Epson salt and water ready in the living room for me to put my feet into after parades and football games. She'd help me out of my uniform and put my casual clothes on, which usually were corduroy pants and a shirt that slipped over my head.

She prepared Thanksgiving dinner all day in those days.
Fronie and Aunt Mae usually came by. Fronie was Daddy's first cousin. We ate in the dining room. We all smiled and talked of pleasant things. They told me how well I did and bragged on Mother's cooking. They usually stayed the day. After dinner, sometimes Daddy went hunting. The home was warm; we had a stove in the living room and many small electric heaters throughout the house. Everyone I was around was pleasant almost all the time.

Mother was an active mother. She enrolled me in tap and ballet classes. She drove me to Stevenson, Alabama, a small town eight miles from where we lived, once a week for lessons. I was in the Brownies and attended meetings once a month. I sold cookies. It was fun. Mother cleaned our home, cooked our meals, washed our clothes, and drove me anywhere I had to go.

I remember when Rudder was in the second grade he told Mother that she was pretty. We were very fortunate to have such good parents that cared for us.

Mother enjoyed visiting her Aunt Nancy in Richard City, Tennessee. Nancy owned and operated an antique shop. She lived in a two-story home. She and Mother called it "the old home place." At least it was one of them.

I spent the night with Carolyn, Mother's cousin. Aunt Katie was Carolyn's mother and Mother's aunt. Carolyn wanted me to stay one night at her grandmother's home. Moma Kirkpatric is what Carolyn called her. She was Aunt Katie and Mamie's mother, Mother's grandmother on her mother's side. She lived in the old home place. It was an old log home next to a mountain.

A long dirt road led to the old log home. When we arrived, Carolyn and I put our clothes in one of the bedrooms. There were big poster beds with a lot of blankets on them. There was a fireplace in most of the rooms as well.

Moma Kirk was tall and lean. She had white hair and wore it in a bun on the back of her head. She was friendly and knew Carolyn. We had a large country supper before going to bed. The bedrooms were cold, but we covered up with the blankets. The fireplace burned with orange and red flames, and I slept well.

The next day, Carolyn filled my glass with orange juice and prepared my breakfast. Moma Kirk ate with us.

Carolyn told her, "She was to keep me for my parents."

Moma Kirk said, "Your mother is my granddaughter." Then she said to Carolyn, "Come and see me any time."

I enjoyed the visit. Moma Kirk said that Mother and her parents lived with them for a year when Mother was young. She said that she loved Peggy (my mother).

The home was old and located on many acres of farmland. We could have walked to the mountain.

Moma Kirk said, "Sometimes wild bobcats come off the mountain. There was a rifle in the kitchen."

We left the home to go down the long driveway. It was a dirt road with a wire fence on both sides. Farmland was all around the area. Although the area was reclusive, it was a pleasure to see my great-grandmother on my mother's side. From my understanding, Moma Kirk had several children: Nancy, Benton, Frances, Katie, and Mamie. Also a half-sister and brother Jerry Kirkpatric.

Mother visited Aunt Nancy a lot. We enjoyed going with her. Her two-story home was full of antiques. Aunt Nancy was an immaculate housekeeper. She even had some family antiques. For instance, she showed us Mother's baby carriage.

Aunt Nancy made delicious homemade peanut butter candy. Almost every time we visited, she made the candy for us. Her living room had large windows; the light came in during the daytime. Mother liked to visit her. She was nice to us and Mother said she enjoyed sitting in the living room. We were always served iced tea as well.

One day Mother took us with her, Rudder and me, to see her mother. She opened the door and the room was shaded from the light. She was watching TV.

"Come in," she said. "I have just made some chocolate pie."

She served us some of the delicious pie. We then sat and watched TV with her. *Librachie* was her favorite program.

Grandmother Mamie and Granddady Lawrence stayed with us a lot when Mother and Dad went on vacations. She was kind to us and he was too. We felt safe and cared for when they visited and stayed with us.

I visited Aunt Mae a lot after the new additions to the family were all born. Daddy would call Aunt Mae and tell her I was coming to see her. Most of the time, she, Fronie, and Annalizbeth would be on the front porch to greet me.

Janice, age nine, sitting on the lawn of Aunt Mae's home.
In one of the dresses she made for me.

I attended school with Aunt Mae. Rash School was a small rural school just outside of Stevenson, Alabama, which consisted of one large room. Most of the grade school children were from rural farm areas. The school also had a cafeteria. I sat with Aunt Mae by her desk. She talked to the children about their lessons. They also read some for her.

Soon it was lunchtime. The ladies wore nets on their hair. I could smell the wonderful food. After school we took a small girl who lived nearby home. I swung on the old tire hung on a tree with rope in the yard.

Aunt Mae liked to knit by her picture window. I sat on her lap as she knit some. She would get up periodically to check on dinner for the family. I noticed her mother's ring as I played with her loose skin on the back of her hand. She was wonderful to me. She told me that she loved me several times when I was with her. She kissed me on the cheek a lot. I enjoyed the stories she told me at night. I remember the little train that didn't think it could get up the hill. "'I think I can, I think I can,' then it did. If you think you can do something you really want to do, 'you can, you can, you can,'" she said.

Aunt Mae was amazing to watch. She cleaned her home, taught school, cooked fine meals, tended her farm, and raised Fronie and Annalizbeth.

We went on many picnics on Flat Rock Mountain. Mrs. Kathryn Riggs went with us. We always packed a basket lunch. We sat on a flat rock near a stream. There are flat rock streams with running water all over Flat Rock Mountain. Annalizbeth would spread out a tablecloth and then spread out the fried chicken, deviled eggs and baked beans. We ate and then waded in the beautiful running water. We talked about how we enjoyed the good food and sometimes talked of David, Mrs. Riggs' son.

Jo John, drinking a pop. Annelizebeth facing front. And me behind her,
and Fronie feeding Jerry. At a picnic on Flat Rock Mountain.

"He wants to be a pilot," she said. "One day a plane flew over our home. David told me, 'I will fly a plane one day.'"

Aunt Mae was friends with all the teachers in the area. She and her family were social.

I can remember the rolling store at Aunt Mae's. One morning, Aunt Mae called me to come out and go through the rolling store. It was a van full of bread and many other food items for the rural areas. I went through it with her and we bought several items, such as bread and flour, sugar and meal.

One day I watched Aunt Mae wring a chicken's neck. She grabbed the chicken and swung it round and round until the chicken had no neck or head. It ran around the yard for a minute before it fell. She then cleaned it and cut it up for frying.

Aunt Mae made many dresses for me. She did fine sewing. I could taste cinnamon and sugar every time she fitted me for a new dress, which were beautiful to me. She bought me some Roman shoes. They were dress shoes with buckles up past my ankles.

Aunt Mae was a small woman, but she could do most anything she wanted to.

Daddy bought the house in front of where we lived. It was a small brick home. I watched him one day pushing a grass seeder in the yard. He had some painters paint the trim work on the brick home. They also painted the inside of the house. I heard Daddy tell Mother, "I plan to rent the home. Then I will sell it." A couple years later, Daddy brought home a new Cadillac. It was blue. We went to Gatlinburg for a family vacation.

The next year we moved up on the hill. We had a two-story home with a view of the Tennessee River. The home had three bathrooms, seven bedrooms, a downstairs kitchen and an upstairs kitchen, a dining room and a living room, and a den downstairs. Daddy purchased some land in the Mud Creek area and built a summer home there.

One day as I was putting books in my locker at junior high school, a blonde, fair, curvy girl touched me on my shoulder. "Hi," she said. "I'm Martha. The band director is short one majorette for the football season. He asked me to find someone. I saw you twirl on TV one time, and I know you were a mascot. If you're interested, be at the band room after school."

I was interested. It was an honor to be a majorette. They were thought of by the students as stars of the school.

I agreed and was at the band room at 2:30 sharp. The majorettes were practicing their routine. Martha introduced me to Mr. Byrd, the band director.

He asked me, "Do you know Judy, Carol, Sue, Brenda, and Linda...and Sandra?" Sandra was the drum majorette.

I said, "Yes, I know them. I've seen them at football games."

They all smiled at me. He then said, "Line up with the other majorettes." I was as tall as most of the others. He smiled. "Martha tells me you have been a mascot as a child and that you have twirled on a television show."

"Yes," I said, "I have. And I twirl a lot for family and enjoyment."

"Would you do a two-hand spin for me? Then a vertical twirl and throw your baton up in midair and turn around and catch it?"

"Yes, sir, I will." I did the two-hand spin, then a vertical twirl, and turned around while throwing my baton in the air and caught it. They applauded.

"You will do fine," he said.

I was thrilled to be chosen.

All the majorettes were beauties. Linda and Sandra were sisters. They favored Rachel Welch. Carol was a real cutie, a natural beauty with light brown hair. Judy was as pretty as Natalie Wood. Sue reminded me of Doris Day. Brenda was as pretty as the *I Dream of Jeanie* star on TV. Martha was an attractive girl also. She had pretty legs and wore her hair in a ponytail style. They remarked about my appearance. They said I was as pretty as Sandra Dee.

I wore my hair blonde. It was blonde when I was a child. Mother decided to let me bleach it for the summer. We put some spray lightener on it for the summer months. It was blonde at the time. I had my hair lightened more for the football season. We all wore blue velvet uniforms. I was an official member of the majorette squad. Mother bought my uniforms every year. I was popular and had a new set of friends. I enjoyed the band and being part of a special group.

Memories

It was early one summer and I was outside practicing my baton routine. After going through a routine several times, I heard a plane fly over head. I looked up and there it was -- a red and white small plane. It flew back over again. I ran in the house and told my dad. He came running out the door. The plane flew over again. It waved its wings.

"I'll bet that's David Riggs. He's your cousin, Janice."

"Ha, ha," Dad laughed as he held his head back. "Davidhas been flying for many years. He's a pilot for Pan Am. He's here to see his mother."

Kathern Riggs. I remember Mrs. Riggs going on picnics with me and Mae and her family. Aunt Mae told me about Kathern Riggs being our cousin through the Hackworths. Mrs. Riggs' husband divorced her and later married a Colgate heiress. David's uncle is Bobby Riggs the tennis player. Dad loved David, he was his young cousin.

"He'll be up to see us soon, Janice."

Dad went back into the house. He was closing a deal on an insurance policy in the study. I was tired and went into the house for some lemonade.

As I sat on the living room sofa, I looked at the picture of dad and Uncle Bill with George Wallace on the console table. Uncle Bill and Daddy were co-owners in the Williams brothers' Phillips distributorship. Dad was the mayor of our small town and Uncle Bill was a state representative. They did everything together. They were a team. I supposed it was because they lost their father when they were children. Granny was a trooper and she brought them up to be good citizens. Granny was a good mother and grandmother. I loved Granny. She was good to me.

Dad—mayor and businessman.

Dad finished up with the insurance man and joined me for a glass of lemonade. Dad reminded me we were to pack for the summer. We were to spend summer at the lake house.

The next day we left. The house was located on the Mud Creek waterfront. We had a boat and a boathouse. We often cruised the big river to Guntersville Lake. The Browings lived next door to us. Uncle Bill lived just down the street. The Loveladys lived next door to Uncle Bill.

I enjoyed the summers at the lake house. The Mud Creek area was near Scottsboro, Alabama. We all boarded our boat and cruised to Guntersville Lake. The water was choppy on the way. I laid on the front bow as I wanted to get some sun. Daddy steered the boat, while Mother and my two little brothers, Rudder and Brian, sat on deck chairs in the rear of the boat. We all enjoyed the three-hour boat ride.

Upon arriving, we spotted the boat dock for fueling. We docked there and filled up with gasoline. We left the boat there while we ate at the Fish House Restaurant. We all had catfish.

After the lunch, we sat on the restaurant's lawn furniture and watched the many boats. There were sail boats, motor ski boats, and water skiers.

It was fun to go to Guntersville on a day-long trip. It took three hours to get there and three hours to return. On the way back we stopped sometimes at a sandy beachfront to swim and get refreshed. We wore ski jackets and ski belts in the water.

One Sunday morning we got up early and Mother packed a picnic lunch. We took the boat and headed out for South Coon Creek. The real name was Raccoon Creek, but we referred to the area as the local people did and called it South Coon Creek.

We took the boat down the small channel to the big river to the creek. We knew we were close when we saw the bright red and green channel floaters. There was a sandy beach and a big rock. In between the beachfront and the big rock was an underground cave. We often explored the cold underground cave. We could also let down the anchor at the big rock and let down some drinks for the cooling. South Coon Creek was our favorite place to spend a summer day on the water. We took food and drinks and ate in the cabin.

I love to remember those days. The sunset was beautiful on the water. The sun went down like a big orange ball. We had to use our boat lights on the way back to the house.

We swam in Aunt Mourine's swimming pool the next day. She prepared some pimento sandwiches and served some bread and butter pickles. Sara Lovelady lived next door. She came over with her son, Jack. She brought a chocolate pie. It was the best chocolate pie I had ever eaten.

Bun Lovelady and Uncle Bill joined me, my little brothers, Sara, and Aunt Mourine at the pool side for some food and swimming. We spent all day around the pool area. We all enjoyed the food, the sun, and the swimming. My brothers and I were always welcome at Uncle Bill's.

One day when I was down at the lakefront looking at the light reflecting off the water, I heard Mrs. Browing (Thelma) calling me. I looked behind me and she was motioning for me to come to the door of her screened in porch. When I entered the screened-in porch, I was met by Toby their English bulldog.

"How have y'all been doing?" Mrs. Browing asked.

"We've been fine," I said.

Mr. Browing (George) joined us on the porch. He sat in a big rocker also. He was a retired businessman. Dad told me he operated a hosiery mill when he was a young child. Mr. Browing had just retired. He and Mrs. Browning had two daughters, Cynthia and Brenda, who were away at college. Some students went to school during the summer months.

Mrs. Browing brought Mr. Browing and me a chocolate milkshake. As I sipped the shake, I looked at Mr. Browing. He was a handsome man. He was educated and had a rugged complexion. He was balding slightly.

He asked me, "Was the river choppy on your trip to Guntersville yesterday? Your dad saw me out in the front lawn and told me you all went to Guntersville."

"Yes, it was choppy. I got some sun and saw many different kind of boats. Sailboats were all over the river down there."

He smiled and said, "We have a new sailboat."

I looked down at the river's edge and there it was -- a small sailboat.

Mrs. Browing told me, "You can use it sometimes if you want to."

A young man was down at the boat dock. Thelma looked out the door. "Hello, Ed," she said.

Ed said, "Hello. Mrs. Browing. Is Cynthia at home?"

"No," replied Mrs. Browing, "she's away at college. Janice is here."

We walked out the door. Ed wore Bermuda shorts. He was clean-cut and nice.

"Will you take Janice out on the sailboat sometime?"

"Yes," Ed replied as he smiled.

Ed and I got on the boat and set sail. We sailed all around the small lakefront. He maneuvered the boat with the small sail and the direction of the wind. Ed lived just across the island in front of us. Mr. Watt, Ed's dad, had a small cabin on the island. We had fun sailing. He asked me for a date and I accepted.

My room consisted of one wall closet with swirl blue and green carpet. My bed was a French design. A copy of the Renoir girls hung over my headboard in my bedroom. Fancy French lamps occupied a place on my nightstand. A white French telephone was also on my nightstand.

My brothers' room consisted of a wall closet and twin beds with designer spreads and bolster pillows. They both had twin chests to put their clothing in. Just outside of our bedrooms was a long mirror on the wall. We could view ourselves in the full-length mirror. A bathroom was between the two bedrooms. It had yellow tile and the walls were painted turquoise. The bathtub was turquoise and the fixtures were gold.

A sliding glass door opened from the living room onto a patio. The ceiling was cathedral, the wood beams were a dull cherry. The chandelier was also a dull brass. A dull brass twin shield hung over the long console table in the living room. A dull brass map hung over the fireplace. A traditional sofa was used in the living room. The colors were beige, old gold, light brown, and a dull orange color with a nubby fabric. The round rug was a brown and gold mixture. Two dull orange leather chairs with matching ottomans were across from the sofa. Dull brass rods held the nubby beige fabric draperies.

In the kitchen were gray cabinets. They were made of oak with a gray stain. We had an oval rattan table in the kitchen with twin loveseats in front of it. The loveseats were seated in front of the gray rock fireplace.

From the kitchen area we had a hallway to the current dining room. It was a screened in porch before we had it converted into a dining room. The dining room was decorated with a narrow Spanish table and Spanish black leather dining room chairs. The ends of the dining room itself had built-in cabinets. The cabinets were stained a light blue-green. The reason being, the decorator said there was not enough room in the furniture buffet; the cabinets were built-in. The doors of the cabinets were decorated with Spanish design and a dull brass finish. The newly decorated dining room had a wine colored carpet.

The foyer, which was the old entrance of the home, was long and narrow. The foyer ceiling was high. A Spanish coffee table was placed in front of the sliding glass windows with two side chairs that were wine velvet.

Mother and Daddy's bedroom was adjacent to the foyer. When I entered into the bedroom, the carpet was a blue-green swirl. It was fancy. Mother and Daddy's bed was king size. The headboard was French antique with posts. It was baroque. The foot of the bed was a long velvet foot bench. It was tufted. There were two bathrooms -- one for Mother and one for Daddy.

One night I slept with Mother when Daddy was out of town. When I got up from the bed, I turned to my left and into the private bathroom. There were two room-length closets -- one for Mom and one for Daddy. There were two swivel rockers set apart by a table. The comfortable chairs faced the entertainment center. The room was large and spacious. The end of the room was solid glass doors. They opened up onto the patio, around the pool area.

The entire house was beautifully decorated. Mother was pleased with the decorator. Our lake home looked as though it had always been the way it was now decorated.

Granny asked Papa to take me to a parade in nearby South Pittsburgh, Tennessee. It only took about eight minutes to get there. The convertibles were lined up just before entering the streets of the small town. I got out of Papa's station wagon. I saw a red convertible just ahead of me preparing to start in the long parade. There weremany convertibles that day. Four girls could ride in one convertible. I sat in the back on one corner.

We waved to the large crowds along the streets. Down the streets we went toward the South Pittsburgh boat dock. When we arrived, a trailer was wrapped with crape paper. It was to be our stage. There were steps on both sides of the stage. The back view was of the river. There were hotdog stands and a huge crowd standing in front of the stage. Above the crowd was a long lower stand. The judges were on the stand seated in strong metal folding chairs. They were all men dressed in short sleeves. They had on dress pants and dress lace-up shoes. Each judge wore a badge that said, "Judge." They looked important and each one had a tablet. There were about eight judges and twenty-two of us girls and every one was pretty. It was a bathing beauty contest.

Mr. Case, the MC for the evening, announced for us to line up, which we did. Each girl walked up the steps and onto the stage. In the center we did a pivot and turned around. The judges wrote as we were on stage. The top ten were then chosen. I was in the top ten. I was trilled to hear my name called out on the speaker.

The contest was narrowed down to four. My name was called out again. I was so thrilled. It was time for the winners to be called out.

After our names were called out as winners, we all did a pivot and were awarded a dozen red roses and trophies and prizes. I liked the part where all three of us stood together in front of the crowd for pictures.

Janice Williams Hughes; age fifteen. Posing in the water.
Just after placing in a bathing beauty contest in 1962.

I felt honored. We all looked different though. We were all the same size, different looking but beautiful. The paper proved that.

One day at the lake house, Ed called at my door. He wanted me to go out on the boat that day. Mother gave me permission and we left for the day.

I had my bathing suit on and grabbed some clean shorts. We boarded at the boat dock. I wanted to water ski. Dad had taught me how to ski at an early age. I jumped into the smooth water and Ed threw the ski over the side of the boat. I slipped them on. Ed eased in front of me in the small ski boat. I held the rope until the slack was completely out of the rope and got into a skiing position.

Ed asked, "Are you ready?"

I nodded yes. He pulled me up on the skis with full force. I skied all around the islands.

We saw a friend of Ed's, a classmate of his.

Ed wanted to ski too. In fact he wanted to ski with me. Ed tied another ski rope onto the back of his boat. His friend, Jim, boarded the boat and operated it while we skied. I skied on one side of the boat and Ed the other side of the boat.

When we fell, Ed had an idea. He told me to ski beside him. I did, then drop one ski and climb up his back after dropping the last ski. I did proceed to climb with my naked feet up the back of his calves of his legs -- the way professionals do in competitions. I succeeded in dropping first the one ski and then the other. I was almost up around his neck when we lost our balance and fell into the water. My bathing suit top came untied and came down during the fall. Ed was a gentleman and didn't look, so I could pull up my top and re-tie it.

We had on our ski belts and floated in the water. We rode a while in the boat after that as he pulled his friend on skis.

We got hungry, so Ed docked at the barbecue place to eat barbecue sandwiches. The sandwiches tasted good. We sat on the dock for a while and watched the other teenagers water ski.

Later that evening, Ed and some other couples met at Ed's cabin for a party. We played records and danced. We ate coldcuts and drank pop. Some friend had brought the food.

I became fond of Ed after that day and into the night date with him. Ed and I dated a lot after that. He was attending the University of Alabama in Tuscaloosa to obtain a degree in engineering. He later worked on building some of the highways in the area after he graduated.

It was mid-afternoon and I was at school. I felt weak, so I asked my teacher if I could go home. She approved a pass and I left. I remembered it was Granny's time to serve the Lion's Club. She was a member of the Women's Club. She cooked along with some other members. I went to the kitchen and joined them.

She had fried chicken, mashed potatoes, coleslaw, and pinto beans. Bet, the black lady who helped, made a cherry cobbler. I sat down and ate. It was delicious.

I still felt weak, so after Granny cleaned up and took the kitchen help home, she took me to the clinic. We saw our family doctor, Dr. Headrick, who was friendly. Granny and I both liked Dr. Headrick. He was charming and a good doctor.

He prescribed a round of antibiotics and a B-twelve shot. "This treatment will help. She'll be fine, Ruby," he said.

I was very active with the majorette squad and school. I weighed 110 pounds. I was healthy, but becoming a teen. I never fainted. I take that back. I did once when I stuck a needle in my finger. It went all the way through to the nail. I was on my way to wash off the blood after I pulled the needle out and the next thing I knew Daddy was picking me up.

I often helped Mother in the afternoons with dinner.Granny and I decided to make an afghan that afternoon. She had started making granny squares. We sat in the living room and made the orchet squares. It took most of the afternoon. I made four. Granny made eight. "We'll sew them together after we have enough for an afghan."

I spent the night with Granny. I slept in the front bedroom in the cherry poster bed. I felt at home there. There was a picture of me on the chest in my majorette uniform. I looked all around the room when in bed.

On the fireplace mantel were lace doilies with antique glass bowls and candles. A cedar chest was at the foot of the bed. Sheer curtains hung on the three windows in the room. Shades were pulled down for privacy. A beautiful floral rug was almost to the floor's edge. The floor was waxed to perfection. I was in the lap of luxury, safe and well taken care of and loved. I went to sleep.

I was awakened in the morning by Papa. "Get up, sleepyhead," he called.

I got up and, after washing my face in the bathroom, arrived at the kitchen table. I sat down and we ate jelly, scrambled eggs, and toast. We always had fresh orange juice and coffee, too. I got ready in a flash after that and Papa took me to school. I was fit and well, no sign of feeling weak or ill.

I remember my baptism. We had a revival several weeks the night before. It was an evening service. I'll never forget that night. Brother Copeland was our minister then. He was inspired by the visiting ministers some weeks before the service. Brother Copeland delivered a sermon on the afterlife.

Hell is for eternity if you choose not to accept the gospel. God is love. God (Jehovah) sent his only son to be born of a virgin Mary. To live here on earth to do his father in heaven's will. Jesus died on a cross for our sins.

I understood that if I became a Christian, I must confess this before the congregation and be immersed in the water to become a new person in Christ.

After the sermon, I walked up to the front when they sang *Come Just As You Are*. I was ready. I knew death came as a thief in the night sometimes. We have no promise of tomorrow, a visiting preacher said.

I was baptized that evening with a wet head in a ponytail style. Several members shook my hand after the service. I was a Christian, and I am a Christian. I will always be a Christian. I love the Lord and try to keep his commandments. I was inspired by Granny who took me to church and bought my first Bible. She will be in heaven when I get there some day and we will see each other again. Granny is gone now, but her memory lives on in my heart. A grandmother is important to her grandchildren.

My Grandmother, Ruby Parton

I am a member of the Church of Christ. Without God, we are lost. I did not want to be without God in my life. After you hear the gospel, you want to be saved. I wanted to remember God when I was young after attending church services frequently. I thought about my salvation and wanted to be baptized. I remember my Sunday school teacher telling me how important it is to read the Bible daily. I can remember all the Church of Christ's ministers we've had over the years that I've attended.

The first preacher I remember as a young teen was Brother Killem, then Brother Copeland. I also remember Brother Barnes and Brother Ross. We had several ministers over the years.

God wants us to come together on the first day of the week to remember Him. We must try to keep his commandments.

We are known by our fruitfulness. In other words, if we
bear fruit, we are Christians. If the people around us want to become Christians, then it is
because of our influence. We share God's word if we are Christians. We want others to become
Christians. As Christians, we want everyone we know to become Christians also. We want to
bear fruit. We want to take someone to heaven with us.

I remember Halloween at Granny's house. October 31st was Granny's birthday.
I was at Granny's and it was almost time for the trick-or-treaters. I was to sit on the
porch and give out candy.

All the kid's started at the foot of the hill. Battery Hill was the place to go for
kids -- it was the safest place in town. There were spooks, witches, tinmen, and all the
spooks. I gave out Hershey chocolates, MilkyWay candy bars, chewing gum and some
hard wrapped candy.

The kids came by in the night. At nine o'clock Papa said, "Turn out the lights."
I did just that.

I wanted to go around myself. I put on a cut-out sheet, overdid some light makeup,
and walked to the houses next door. I went to Mrs. Loyd's house. She had made some
popcorn balls. She also gave me some of the delicious homemade treats. I thanked her
and was on my way to another house. I stopped at a home that gave homemade mound
candy bars. Mary, the lady of the house, gave me two saran-wrapped bars. I went over
to Betty Jo's, dad's cousin. She was a natural beauty. She was a refined woman that I'd
never met as a child. I heard Aunt Myrtle tell us how wonderful her daughter was. She
was from Texas, well traveled, and educated. I enjoyed looking at Betty Jo. She had

dark brown hair and her voice was soft. She was a small woman. I always noticed her earrings when I saw her. They dangled, and like no others I had ever seen. They were purchased by her husband from his travels.

She had homemade treats, also divinity candy and marshmallow crispy treat balls. I thanked her and decided to go back to Granny's.

"It's time to go to bed," Granny said. I begged her to let me stay in the living room and watch TV. She told me to keep the volume low. I did and ate my goodies. I watched scary movies until midnight.

The next day, we sat on the front porch. The leaves were at their peak. Bright orange and yellow trees were all around us. Some were also a red plum color.

The day was beautiful and surprisingly warm. We were in a most beautiful area on Battery Hill. Papa sacked up all the fallen leaves after lunch that day. Granny cooked homemade stew for supper. For desert was peach cobbler and ice cream. Uncle Bill and Aunt Mourine came by to eat with us. We ate heartily. "We didn't have any down on the lake," Uncle Bill said.

There were not many people with small children down on the lake area. Uncle Bill and Aunt Mourine stayed on the lake year round. They had modernized their home as Dad did with weatherizing and fireplaces. We could stay at the lake all year round.

Granny opened her birthday gifts after supper. She got a blouse, a raincoat from Papa, and a bottle of perfume from me. It was a nice holiday and birthday for me and my family.

It was seven o'clock in the morning. Dad got up early and fixed country ham and homemade biscuits. Mother fried the scrambled eggs. We, for once, had time to eat breakfast before going to school.

After the good meal, Dad took us to school. Rudder, Brian and I went to different parts of the school. I was in high school. Rudder and Brian went to grade school. It was a Friday. I knew that evening that I would be performing on the football field.

I was at the bandroom by six-thirty that evening, just in time to go through our routine. We put glitter in our hair. It was a big night for us. We were playing Stevenson, A1, our rival. The drummer started the drum cadence. His name was Bob Lee; we got to know one another on the band bus going to out of town games. I liked him. He was a smart fellow with a good voice. He was blond and tall. We were friends.

We lined up to enter the stands. Our uniforms were blue velvet. Granny took me to *Button and Badge* to have mine made. The band director started a number the band played until the game started.

A player's name was called out. It was Marron, one of the Tony twins. There were two: Arron and Marron. Well, they were tall and built well. They had good dispositions. They were liked by all the teens. They both had deep voices.

Afterwards, the Stevenson cheerleaders went down to lead the opposing team off the field. Ours did the same for our team. We left the stands with a cadence from Bob. We lined up at the goal line. We marched up eight marching steps, then three lines up. The band was behind us. We then marched to the opposing side to perform.

It was a thrilling night. We twirled fire batons. It was on our side, we were brought the baton filled with kerosene. Then they were lit, we did a flash, then a two-hand spin. We threw the fire batons up into the air, then we did a repeat until the band number was over.

We won that night. After the game was over, I walked one of the players off the football field. He had asked me earlier at school. He was so cute. He had blond hair. His name was Leonard, and we liked one another. We saw each other from time to time. We talked on the phone and went to some parties together. He gave me a gold heart pendant. We accompanied each other to the town movie theater. The courtship lasted about a year, then we became interested in other sweethearts. The season passed quickly.

It was March and there was talk of the wedding. Cynthia was getting married. Mrs. Bowning told me this when I was in Mecllan's Pharmacy picking up some medication for Mother.

Soon the big day came. The wedding was at two o'clock on a Saturday afternoon. I was at church early that day. I sat by Linda Rankin, a classmate of mine -- she played the clarinet in the band. She was Cynthia's cousin. After some piano music, the bridal march started. Cynthia was accompanied by her dad down the aisle. She wore a long lace trimmed wedding gown. Her hair was back away from her face. Her wedding hat had a short train of thin material attached to the back of it. She was elegant looking; the dress looked as if it had been made for her.

I enjoyed the wedding and the day's activities. It the event of the year for our social circle.

I remember the snow during Christmas on Battery Hill. It was a cold day in December. The weatherman predicted snow of four to six inches. We had fun as we slid down the banks and made snow cream. We slid down the left side of the hill on a sled ordered by Dad. It was a big red one. Teens would line up from as far back as a block to take the ride down the high slide. Practically no cars came around the hill after a deep snowfall. We had a fun holiday whenever a big snow fell. It was a two-week vacation that year because of the high snowfall.

Everyone was friendly during snow time. Mother always served hot chocolate to our visitors. It was so pretty to wake up and see the front lawn covered in snow. It looked like a greeting card all around the hill. I wore boots when I walked to Granny's house. We had a fire built upstairs and downstairs in our split-level home when it snowed in our little town of Bridgeport, Alabama.

When spring came with its flowers blooming all around the hill, we forgot all about the winter snow. There were more dogwood trees around the hill, pink ones and white ones. All the buttercups and tulips were in full bloom in April.

It is relatively warm here in our area of Alabama. We enjoy the changing of the seasons. The mountains are huge and the river is beside us. We are centrally located in our little valley. The beautiful historical homes on the hill are over 100 years old. It's like going back in time when you view them all in our environment.

Bluebirds fly all around the hill, as well as redbirds and hummingbirds fly up on our decks and back porches.

We can see the river from our back windows. To the left are hills and farmland up into Tennessee. On a clear day we can even see the river bridge in nearby South Pittsburg, Tennessee.

A big gray rock marks the point of our hill. Three small trees, six-feet side by side, mark the bottom of the hill's entrance. One may go around to the right or to the left. The North and South fought on the point. A cannon lies on the bottom of the river near the bridge. Arrowheads can also be found all around the hill. It's no surprise to have someone knock on your door and ask if they hunt for mini balls. A few years ago, someone found some bones of a soldier. The place was roped off and the remains were sent to Auburn for study. We think of the beauty of the hill and the mountains, however, it is also a historical site.

Christmas at Granny's house. Everyone arrived at about six-thirty on Christmas Eve. We put all our gifts under the tree. Granny always had a silver tree in the foyer of her beautiful 100-year-old restored home. We sat in the living room until she came in to tell us dinner was ready. We then filed into the dining room table -- my two brothers, Brian and Rudder, and I. Sometimes my little brother who was retarded was there. He was always away most of the time at a school for the retarded. We entertained him through the years on the holidays at different times. He was there, as were Uncle Bill and Aunt Mourine, and Mother and Daddy.

We sat down to eat. Granny had a mahogany dining room suite. It was a large table. We ate from rose-colored floral border china. The rose crystal glasses were filled with tea. A huge turkey was served. We had green beans, mashed potatoes, and cranberry salad. Granny liked to fix the salad rather than the smooth canned cranberry. She would cook the whole cranberries, add pecans and jell it for an hour before serving. She cut up squares to serve over lettuce with a meal. I especially liked Granny's dressing. She made it with cornbread and mixed it with onions, celery, and a few other spices. She always had turkey gravy. It was served in a gravy boat of her china. We had a feast.

After dinner we were served dessert. We had different kinds for different holidays. We had strawberry cake, cherry cobbler with ice cream and, my favorite, coconut and chocolate pie. Granny was an excellent cook. Papa spared nothing for a fine dinner on a holiday. He was generous with Granny about money.

After dinner, Aunt Mourine and I helped Granny clean the table of the china and silverware. We then retired to the living room for the opening the gifts. We all gathered around and sat in a circle. I was in charge of getting the wrapped gifts from under the tree. I would call out the names and give out the gifts.

That year, Shelly, my little retarded brother, got some toy guns. I called out his name first. "Shelly," I said as I gave him the gift. He tore into the wrapping. When he saw it was toy guns, he immediately put them on. They had a belt. I then called out the other names for the family.

Before the night was over, all the gifts were opened and admired. I enjoyed my gifts from everyone. I usually got a sweater from Granny, a money envelope from Aunt Mourine and Uncle Bill. Sometimes Aunt Mourine got me a sweater outfit also. I remember her calling to ask if I would like to go shopping. Mother and Daddy got me an amethyst ring that year set in yellow gold. It was a twin amethyst -- one stone set on top of the other. I got excited over jewelry. I enjoyed the Christmas Eves at Granny's.

I remember the years Dad owned a bowling alley. He was offered some property near Kimball, Tennessee. It was a good deal, so Dad took the offer. A large bowling alley was built. John Denton was the manager of the new business. Mr. John Denton was the husband of dad's cousin, Betty Joe. He was small of stature and slightly bald, with big white teeth. He smiled a lot. He was an intelligent man and well educated. Dad was impressed with John because of John's optimistic personality. John always smiled and waved at us when he saw Rudder and me. Dad decided he would be good for the business and was pleased with John's ability as the manager of the bowling alley.

There were bowling lanes and locker space. I was in a bowling league. I met a lot of young teens from Tennessee. I learned to bowl. My scores ranged from 250 to 280. I was an excellent bowler. We had a teacher to show us teens how to bowl. *Big John* was a famous song at the time. I can remember hearing the song on the jukebox when I bowled. The bowling alley lasted many years. Finally, Daddy sold the property.

Daddy bought and sold property a lot. He and Uncle Bill would get a tip on some property being close to a new highway and purchase it. It wasn't long before Uncle Bill and Daddy became millionaires. I always thought it was because granddaddy took his own life and that made them try harder to make it in this life. They were both successful at whatever they did.

Dad wore different hats when he opened a new business. I can remember him being in the paper as the man with the Midas touch. He wore a hardhat with bowling pins attached to it for the paper. However, most of his life, he wore a Texas western hat with his suits. A shopping center in the Stevenson area was built on some property Dad and some of his business associates owned. He was in partnerships with a lot of businessmen.

While Daddy had the bowling alley, I met many teens on a bowling league. One Thursday after school, I got a call from a South Pittsburgh boy. He asked me out to a party for young teens. It was at a cabin on the South Pittsburgh Lake. I accepted and we attended the party. It was crowded on the dance floor, however, I enjoyed the fun and company. All the young beautiful people were there. While I was dancing, I noticed a handsome young South Pittsburgh football player, blond and popular. He bumped into me and our eyes met. He was cute, but I was with someone else.

My date and I danced the night away. Refreshments were served by the parents of the teen having the party: Cokes, cookies, and sandwiches. I felt older and in with the in-crowd. No one from Bridgeport was there. I was accepted by the Tennessee group. I thought it was because of the bowling alley. Many of them were on the bowling league.

I loved to dance and danced with several boys there. I smiled and talked with several girls from the area: Kathy Carter, Susan Headrick, Carolyn Havron, Susan Kellerman, Rusty Adcock. The night passed too quickly. Buz brought me home.

I frequented a few more parties in Tennessee, but I did not get serious with any boy from the area.

My parties at home consisted of band banquets and football games. There wasn't much to do at home except go to the dairy bar or to a movie.

Dad informed us he had some tickets to the Alabama football game in Birmingham. Saturday morning we left for Legion Field in Birmingham, Alabama. We stopped on the way down to the game to have breakfast at a nice restaurant. I ordered poached eggs and country ham and biscuits.

Dad laughed at me for eating so much and weighing only 110 pounds. He talked about the Alabama coach, Bear Bryant, being a great coach. Dad told me that he read in it the newspaper that Bear had the Alabama players take a semester of ballet. He said, "That would make them more graceful." Dad laughed as he told us.

We arrived at Legion Field at about 1:00 in the afternoon. Our seats were halfway to the top of the stands. I could see the green field and white lines clearly from our seats.

As I looked all I could see the stadium was full of people. The Alabama cheerleaders were just down from us. The bands were in the stands. Excitement was everywhere.

The announcer's voice came over the speaker. "Let us all stand and recite the Pledge of Allegiance to the flag."

Everyone stood up and put their hands over their hearts and faced the flag while reciting the Pledge of Allegiance.

The game started after we sat down. The opposing team won the toss. After the kickoff one of Alabama's players caught the ball and ran several yards before being tackled near the goal line. Alabama was so close, but they decided to kick the ball to make a score. The kick was good as the ball went over the goal post. Everyone got up and cheered.

After Alabama scored the first point the opposing team made several scores in their favor.

The majorettes wore crimson red sequenions. They also wore tall white boots. The band marched up the field behind the majorettes. As the band played, they maneuvered in positions to represent a guitar while playing "Rock Around the Clock." The majorettes twirled a baton while dancing. I enjoyed the halftime show.

The players entered the field after the halftime show. Bear Bryant waved his hand and talked with a lot of serious expressions to the Alabama players. Joe Namath caught the ball and ran down the field until he sighted another Alabama player that caught the pass and ran a touchdown.

"Roll, Tide, roll," cheered the fans.

Dad got up and screamed, "Yaaa! Yaaa! Ye! He! Ye! He!"

After the play the opposing team couldn't make another touchdown due to Alabama blocking their runners. "Joe" was throwing the ball again as he looked for a receiver. Then Joe noticed a free way to the goal line. Touchdown Namath it was. Dad got up and screamed with extreme joy.

The Alabama Crimson Tide made several more scores to win the game. After the last play, Dad got up and screamed, "Ye! Ye! Ye! He! Ye! He!" He smiled like I had never seen before.

After we got into our car, Dad told us we would be dining at one of Birmingham's most popular restaurants. We dined at Joy Youngs. We ordered Oriental cuisine. The waiter took our order and called it back to us in order. We were impressed. I especially liked the egg rolls dipped in sweet-and-sour sauce.

After the excellent dinner, we got in our brand new car. Dad had just bought it a few weeks before the game. Dad told Rudder and me to buckle in. He said he heard Ralph Nader say on television that safety belts were not being used.

We headed toward home. I could smell the newness of the leather seats. I could hear Mother and Daddy discussing the day's events. The ride was smooth. I felt full and happy.

I remember dating Ed Watt and going to Chattanooga to a plush nightclub dinner spot on Lookout Mountain with a view of Chattanooga. It was the Panorama Club. Ed was a college guy and knew how to treat a girl to a night out on the town. I liked Ed.

Ed picked me up at 4:00 sharp. We were on our way to Lookout Mountain to pick up Frank and Virginia Car. They were going to go with us to the Pan-O-Ram Club on the mountaintop for dinner. The club was the nightspot for the social elect.

After arriving at the Car's home, Ed and I sat on the sofa while Virginia finished getting ready. Ed introduced me to them in the living room. I remembered Virginia. She had been a majorette when I was a mascot for our band. She was pretty and Frank was handsome, educated, and wealthy. He had graduated from college and was working in Chattanooga. Frank and Virginia were newlyweds and were happy. They were smiling and ready for a fun evening.

After we entered the nightclub, Frank had the waiter seat us in front of the huge windows overlooking the city of Chattanooga. It was a beautiful view of a lighted city.

Virginia danced with Ed. I was sitting at the table with Frank. He said, "You have beautiful eyes." I thanked him for the compliment. We drank the champagne from the long-stem glasses. "Ed is a nice fellow," Frank said as we looked at the view from the window.

Frank's father was the president of the bank where I lived. Ed's mother worked at the bank. Frank, Ed and Virginia had attended high school together.

I danced some with Ed. We held each other close. I was a young teen, but I looked 21 that evening in my evening attire.

A few weeks later, Ed asked me to attend a weekend trip to Knoxville to attend the Alabama/Tennessee game.

Dad decided to break up this courtship because Ed and I were becoming seriously interested in one another.

The next summer, the majorettes and I were practicing our routine and marches down the football field. I saw Ed at the fence. I ran over to greet him and put my hand up on his at the fence. He told me that he was in for a few days. We talked, but when he left, I knew it was goodbye. Daddy was right, Ed was a man and I was a girl. I needed more time, I thought, to attend football games and parties. To chew bubble gum, skip jump, and comb my hair and primp a lot in front of the mirror.

One day during Christmas vacation, I was out at the oil company. Dad had hired a young man from Bridgeport named John Hughes. John had dropped out of Auburn to help with his family's finances. He applied for clerical work at the oil company.

I smiled at him. Dad asked him to pick up my retarded brother from Murfreeburrow. We went together and got to know one another. John Hughes was six years older than I. He and I picked up Shelly from the retarded home for Christmas at home, he was waiting in the foyer when we got there and ready to go. He sang *City Lights* all the way home.

Thanksgiving at Aunt Mae's with Aunt Mae and her two daughters, Annelizebeth and Saphrona. Aunt Mae was a small woman. She had reddish-brown hair. Her sweet small face was full of freckles. She sang my name when she called me to help her make cinnamon rolls. I loved her. She was granddaddy Rudder's sister. She taught grammar school.   Fronie, as we called her, was married to John McGraw and they had two boys. Jo, John, and Jerry. Fronie named them after Daddy and Uncle Bill. Annelizebeth was married to Rice Coffee.

Rice Coffee, as I remember, was a small-framed man; he had a deep voice and smoked cigarettes. I remember him admiring Annelizebeth when she combed her dark brown hair. Her ankles were small, her legs were long, and her nails were painted. Aunt Mae said she was ready for college at the age of fifteen. She obtained a bachelor of science degree from college and taught school for a while. Ann designed a horseshoe drive at the side of Aunt Mae's home. She then planted a flower garden in the center of the driveway.

They did not have any children. Annelizebeth was divorced from Mr. Coffee at the time and was dating a man she knew while in college. Bill was his first name and he was very handsome. He taught school. After his wife had died, he called Ann and told her he remembered how beautiful she was. He asked if she was married. Ann laughed when she told us about it.

Aunt Myrtle and Aunt Mae were sisters. As a child, I remember Aunt Myrtle giving me my first pet. She came to live with Aunt Mae on the farm when I was a child when Mr. Blackmore, her husband and Betty Jo's father, died.

Jet was the small cocker spaniel's name. I called him *jeat*. Annelizebeth told me to say jet, not *jeat*. After some coaching from her, I learned to say jet.

Our cousin Betty Jo and her husband John moved there from Texas a few months after Aunt Myrtle moved in with her sister. John, Betty Jo and Aunt Myrtle lived in a home near us on Battery Hill.

The dining table was set with a cornucopia in the center of the table. It was filled with squash and eggplant. The dishes and crystal were the colors of autumn -- a light brown. The placemats were an orange-leaf color. The table setting reminded us of autumn leaves. A turkey, with cornbread dressing and giblet gravy, was served. We had several vegetables and pumpkin pie or peach cobbler with ice cream, whichever we preferred.

We laughed and talked about our trips to the campgrounds with John, Fronie and the boys. Ann talked about marrying her old acquaintance soon, who knocked at the door just before the meal was finished. He entered the dining room. He looked like Clark Gable to me. I remember seeing he ate some dessert with us.

After dinner, I went upstairs. We called Aunt Mae's home a farmhouse. Upstairs, I lay down in one of the twin beds. I remembered staying with them as a small child. I could remember waking up in the night and Fronie saying, "It's Fronie," and covering me up with a quilt. I also remember sleeping in the big bedroom with Aunt Mae. She would tickle my back until I went to sleep. I had memories of lying on the floor in the summer and looking out the window in my nightgown and listening to the crickets make their "wa, wou" sound. I was filled with wonderment when I was a child and to me every sound was a marvelous sound.

I felt rested and then went downstairs to join the family. They had gone outside on the porch. I went and opened the door. In the backyard, Rudder was petting a cow. I joined him. She stuck her head in between the wooden fence. Her face was white and her fur was curly. She was tame. We enjoyed seeing the cow and eating dinner with Aunt Mae and her family -- a family we felt very much a part of.

It was the month of February. Mother and Dad were out of town on a business trip. It was a dull month for me. I had been dating John Hughes for six months. All of my friends had graduated from high school. I wanted to marry John. He seemed nice enough. John's family attended the church that I belonged to. His family was well thought of in the community. John's father worked as an electrician in a nearby plant. His mother was a homemaker.

Sue and Wendell Smith were friends in high school. Sue had been a majorette when we had gone to camp together. She was about two years older than me. She had a freckled face, and cute as she could be. Wendell was an all-American guy. He was always smiling. I had known she and Wendell as girlfriend and boyfriend. They fell in love and got married.

After they were married, I visited Sue one day at her mother-in-law's. She was folding clothes. I asked her to go with John and me to Georgia.

I knew anyone could marry in nearby Trenton, Georgia in one day. John and I picked up Sue and Wendell and drove to nearby Trenton.

There we went to the courthouse to get our blood tests and marriage licenses. After the tests, we were told of a preacher that lived just up the road from the courthouse. We found the small brick home and got out of the car. John knocked on the door. The preacher was smiling as he opened it. "Come in, come in," he said.

Suddenly, as we were just about to be married, I realized that we didn't have any rings. Sue took off her wedding band of gold and gave it to me. As the preacher said, "John, will you take this woman to be your lawful-wedded wife," John said, "Yes," as he slipped the gold band on my finger. The preacher then asked me the same question about John. I said yes as I put the ring on his finger.

Sue and Wendell hugged us after the ceremony. We then went out to a small restaurant to eat dinner.

I told John that I would keep the marriage a secret until I graduated from school. I only told two of my classmates -- Mary Jo and Barbara. The word got out that John and I were married. Daddy found out and was upset, to say the least. But he decided not to annul the marriage due to his respect for John's family. After the storm blew over, John and I moved into a new house. It was new to us, anyway. The house was located in Parton Heights, a small Alabama town. It had a living room, a small kitchen, and a bathroom and bedroom upstairs. The house had a basement with a small bathroom in it. The basement was partially furnished. It had potential. We were happy with the house. There were only the two of us.

Daddy told me to do something, so I decided to attend beauty college. I drove to Fort Payne every day for a year. I took the beauty exam in Birmingham and passed the state board of cosmetology. I became a hairdresser.

Soon after I became a hairdresser, I was expecting a baby and was overdue. I was supposed to deliver on March 12, 1965. However, April 1 came and no baby. I was given a drip to induce labor by Dr. James Havron, a M.D. who learned how to do surgeries in the army. Dr. Havron was a small, friendly man who liked to fish in his spare time. Dad knew him; he fished near our summer home on the lake.

I was in labor all day and into the night. I slapped the attending nurse and called my husband a son of a bitch.

Dr. Havron decided to do a caesarian section and deliver my baby. On April 1, 1965 at 9:00 a.m., I was wheeled in the operating room. Dr. Havron stuck me with a tiny pin to see if I was numb from the spinal. He asked me if I felt it. No, I hadn't when he stuck my stomach. "Do you want to be awake or asleep?" he asked.

I was just seventeen and frightened. I could see the huge light over me and several of the doctors with green hats and white masks on. He administered some anesthetic to put me under.

As I awoke, Dr. Havron was standing over me in the recovery room. He was wearing his green hat and his mask was partly on. He tapped my face with his hand and asked me if I was all right. I nodded up and down.

"You have a healthy baby girl," he said, smiling. He then told the attending nurse to observe me for about thirty minutes then roll me in my room.

After a few minutes and a cold face washing and a drink of water I was rolled into my hospital room. Granny, daddy, Uncle Bill, Aunt Mourine, and my husband were there. I could feel the many kisses on my cheeks as I lay half-awake in my bed.

The nurse brought my baby girl in. She weighed 9 pounds and 11 ounces, and was 22 inches long. I held her and gave her a bottle. I felt glad she was here and the delivery by c-section was over.

Granny said, "This baby has given me a new lease on life." She smiled and then asked me what I was going to call her.

"Suzanne," I told her. I liked the name. Peggy was my mother's name and since it was customary for southern people to name their first girl baby after their mother, Peggy Suzanne it was. Suzanne was what we called her.

John and I had been married only a few years when Dad called me to meet him at the office. John informed me that we were to wear dress clothing. He told me about the parade and George Wallace coming to the Stevenson Airport to meet some of the local people. It was close to election time.

I had a new dress for spring. It was a fuchsia dress trimmed in navy. I also wore navy pantyhose. I wore my hair in a pageboy long shoulder length. As we entered Dad's office, Uncle Bill was smiling there. They asked John and me to sit down. Dad was sitting behind the desk smoking a cigar. He was dressed in a suit and had his western hat on.

I noticed Lurleen's picture hanging on the wall behind Dad's desk. She was wearing a hunter's outfit and holding a bird. She had given Dad the picture when she was the governor. I believe the picture was sent out to supporters to show she had the strength to become governor.

Dad took a draw off his cigar and let it go. "As you all know Lurleen died of cancer some time back," he said. "George is married to Cornelia now. She's a beautiful young woman. Cornelia's uncle was Big Jim Folsome. She was also as a young woman a water skier for the Cypress Garden's show in Florida. George and Cornelia will be at the Stevenson Airport in just a few minutes." There was to be a parade in Stevenson to welcome Mr. Wallace.

When we arrived at Stevenson the parade was marching down the front streets. It was Stevenson's high school band, dressed in full uniform. I saw Mr. Wallace shaking hands beside some of the marching band. Dad and I crossed the street together.

"George," Dad said as we walked up to him.

"Jay," said Mr. Wallace. They shook hands.

"George, I want you to meet Janice, my daughter."

Mr. Wallace smiled at me as he put his arm around me and shook my hand firmly. "Hello, darlin'," he said. He was a handsome man. He smelled as if he had washed in the finest deodorant soaps and rinsed to perfection and his breath was as fresh as the mountain air. He had a faint gardenia smell. It was a masculine smell, but sweet. Daddy always wore Old Spice. That's why I noticed the wonderful smell of Mr. Wallace's cologne. His tie was red and his suit was navy.

After we met, Dad asked me to go into the stores in this small town and ask the proprietors to vote for Wallace on voting day. As I entered the stores, I asked the people to vote for Wallace. They smiled and shook their heads up and down as to say, yes they would.

When I left the last store, I saw Mrs. Wallace from a distance. Cornelia wore a red dress. Her hair was short and medium brown. She was smiling and shaking hands.

The day was a big event for me. George Wallace was elected that year for governor. He helped our small town in getting the roads paved.

The home, the land, the church, the politics, and the family helped make me what I am.

The Young Married Years

I was at home with the newborn. Mother came by with Bet, the African-American helper we had all my young life. Mother was trying to make it easy for me. I had a cesarean section and was not supposed to lift heavy objects. I was also not to vacuum the floor, mop, or overdo myself. Bet was a much-needed asset to me.

All the newborn needed was a bottle and changing and bathing. For a whole month, I had help with our baby. When I was on my own I noticed her reactions. She made a loud sound when she awoke at night and then she would listen for me. That meant she was an intelligent baby.

I was happy that she was not like my brother, Shelly. I remembered what a hardship he was on my mother before Daddy sent him to retard boarding school. Suzanne walked on time; she talked on time.

Granny helped me with her so I could work in the beauty shop. I was a hairdresser and quite successful at the profession. John had purchased the small shop, Marie's Beauty Shoppe. Usually it took five years to build up a business, however, because of the clientele already patronizing the business, it didn't take as long. I had worked previously at a shop in town, and one in nearby Stevenson, Alabama. I had some customers of my own.

I attended beauty shows and kept up to date on current hairstyles by reading the hairstyle magazines. Once you become a hair stylist, you can attend a hair show for beauticians and watch a hairstylist from New York or Atlanta do his or her new hairstyles. It was a good profession. I cut, permed, tinted, and frosted hair from age nineteen to thirty.

John stopped working for my father at the oil company soon after Suzanne was born. Dad had separated the oil company from the trucking business. Uncle Bill stayed and operated the oil company while Dad moved his trucking business to Florida. John purchased a small furniture and appliance business from a relative. He excelled at selling heating and cooling units, chainsaws, lawnmowers, televisions, and furniture and appliances.

He won a trip to Las Vegas, Nevada. It was a most enjoyable trip. We had a few meetings in one of the hotel's banquet rooms and dinners were on the vendor. We saw Johnny Cash one night in the hotel's entertainment center. We ate in the hotel's restaurants and gambled on the many slot machines. We only stayed three days, but we enjoyed the bright lights, the entertainment, and meeting with the other storeowners.

Not long afterwards, John won another trip. This one was to Hawaii for a full week in Honolulu. I was thrilled as I had always wanted to go to Hawaii. Granny agreed to keep Suzanne and the following week we were off to Hawaii with the homebuilders.

The flight took ten hours. We touched down in Honolulu and were met by hula girls with flower leis. They wrapped the leis around our necks as we left the plane's landing steps. We were taken by bus to our motel. It was a sunny, breezy day. We had jet lag, so we slept and rested for a day before touring the island.

After we rested, we took a tour of the island. Our guide informed us when we passed some of the native Hawaiian homes. The homes of the native Hawaiians cannot be sold to Americans; United States citizens but through one lifetime. That's what the tour guide said! It goes back to Hawaii. We rode by the famous blowhole, a rock formation at the edge of the ocean and the ocean came up through a hole in the rock. The ocean spewed from the hole in two directions. It was as pretty as a fountain, a natural fountain.

We drove by *Hawaii 50's* star's home and then we were bussed by Elvis' home. It was on a bluff overlooking a calm oceanfront. There were two rock formations on each side of the beach in front of the star's ocean view of his home. The rock formations and the middle sea of turquoise was a beautiful sight.

Janice standing by Bill Harrison in Hawaii 50's Star.

We arrived at a garden spot to rest and eat. We enjoyed the many garden flowers and man-made bridges across the gardens and water ponds. We also shopped in the village's shops.

After we left, we were bussed to the island's volcano site.

"It hasn't erupted in years," the tour guide said. "When it does, it changes the terrain." Then he told us of the year it had resulting in many rocky benches and rock formations around the island. I was glad when we left the site.

We had a rocky beachfront at our hotel and had to wear shoes to wade in the beach. The waves were high above my head. Many people in our group rented canoes and paddled along the shoreline far out just after the waves came in. We observed them. There were not many swimmers because of the high waves. Surfers were plentiful though.

The temperature was warm and windy most of the days we were there. One sunny day, some of us went to see the *USS Arizona* memorial. It was a building alongside a dock walk. At the end of the walkway, we looked off the dock at the ocean blue.

"It is here," the tour guide said, "where the *USS Arizona* went down. As you can see, gasoline is still coming up from the wreckage. Our servicemen are entombed in the ship. It was attempted at one time to bring them and the ship up. However, it was too dangerous. Their names are engraved in marble alongside the memorial building."

Many of the island's cars were old. Our tour guide told us, "The cars on the island are shipped in. No cars are made on the island."

We island-hopped one day. The island was different than Honolulu. The beaches were rockier due to the volcanoes. We spent a night in the one hotel on the island. We toured the small village on the island. Shops were everywhere, as were native homes, rulers of a time gone by.

We viewed a parade. There were many convertibles and old Cadillacs with native beauties riding in the backseats. Miss Hawaii was wearing a crown. We waved at her as she rode by in a convertible.

The motel stay was pleasurable. We had a fine meal that evening. The motel's restaurant was outside overlooking the ocean. A small bridge provided a walkway across a huge man-made pond. Huge goldfish filled the pond.

The next day, we all went to a park on the big island of Honolulu. There we had a louaha. A pig was roasted in the ground and a Hawaiian dish was served. It had the consistency of glue. In fact, it tasted like glue. It was called Hawaiian poey. We all said "phooey" with the poey. We enjoyed the pork roast and rum punch while viewing the ocean.

We toured some of the fabric plants. We dined nightly in the hotel's restaurant overlooking the ocean. We had a free day so we walked high atop a view near downtown Honolulu. We ate some coconut ice cream, which was an island favorite.

We left Hawaii rested and pleased with the trip. We didn't have time to see all Hawaii had to offer. One week was just not enough time on the beautiful islands. Aloha to Hawaii. It means goodbye and hello. It is a greeting among the natives. We will never forget Hawaii and the good times we had there.

Suzanne was a little girl. She was intelligent, but had an introverted personality. I decided to enroll her in piano classes. The lady just down the street gave lessons. Suzanne could ride down to piano class on her bicycle. John bought her a new Baldwin piano at my request. I wanted to do everything I could to see that she had a proper upbringing.

An introverted personality just means reserved, not outgoing. However, Suzanne had many good qualities and she was intelligent. College is almost a must for introverted personalities. I knew I would personally see to it that she attended college. When she was older, I enrolled her in art class and she enjoyed painting.

I became active in civic affairs. I became a member of the women's club and soon became its president. Everyone brought their favorite recipes and published a cookbook. The town merchants financed the project. The money earned went to the club.

Suzanne did well in school. She knew music and requested to be in the school band. John bought her a new clarinet. Suzanne enjoyed playing in the band. For several years she played clarinet before deciding she wanted to be a majorette or a drum majorette. She decided to be a drum majorette. She tried out and was approved by the judges. We attended many of the games.

We loved our daughter and both John and myself wanted only the best for her. She didn't have any brothers and sisters. As a result of that, she kept active in school activities.

I wanted more children, however, I only had one baby girl after Suzanne was born. We named her Melody Jeannette. She was stillborn. After the stillbirth of our second child, the fact that I had RH-negative blood type and a Mongoloid brother, I decided not to have any more children.

We took Suzanne to church and Sunday school. She also attended Bible school classes every summer that the church offered. Suzanne accepted Jesus Christ as her savior at an early age and is a born-again Christian. Suzanne was baptized for the remission of her sins and stated in front of the congregation that she believed Jehovah God sent His only son to die on the cross for our sins. She was then baptized in the name of the Father, the Son, and the Holy Ghost. Suzanne was then redeemed and became a member of the church of Christ.

Suzanne finished high school and chose the University of Alabama for college. She finished in four years. She became engaged to a nice young man. She attended

Alabama law school and became an attorney after she passed the Alabama law board.

John excelled at selling in the little store we owned.

When Suzanne was still a child, we went on many

trips. We flew to Bermuda where the motel was right on the oceanfront. Many sailboats were just across from the motel's balcony. I could see the colorful boats and sails on the waterfronts. We dined in the hotel's banquet room. The chefs all wore tall hats. As we entered the banquet room, I could see the huge silver containers of hot food. The chefs were opening the huge silver containers of delicious food to inspect. We ate on long tables lined up for our group and every night we had a fine meal of delicious food. A chocolate mint was on top of our pillow every night.

The weather was warm and mild. The many shops in downtown Bermuda sold perfume and clothing and we toured a shirt and sweater shop. The natives drove on the opposite side of the road there.

I had my hair done at one of the beauty shops. It was a relaxed atmosphere. I was served a beverage. My hairstylist styled my hair well and she also did my nails.

We walked around the island. We came upon a big hotel restaurant. We looked inside and the chef motioned for us to come in.

Lunch had already been served, however, he said, "We have some turkey for some sandwiches, and some soup as well."

We were served turkey sandwiches, a cup of soup, and some delicious cake.

Jamaica was beautiful and exciting to visit. All nationalities were around the swimming pool. We swam all day and ate well too. We turned down a trip to the sugarcane fields to swim and take it easy. Granny and Papa went on the day-long trip. Late that evening, just before dinner, Granny and Papa returned. They came out to the pool area and told us about their trip. It was more than a trip to the sugarcane fields. It was a view of the island homes.

"We had a picnic," she said. "The islands were beautiful."

Granny then made an appointment to get her hair done before dinner. They dined with us that evening. A professional photographer was there taking pictures. We dined on fish and potatoes and salad, as well as green vegetables. The dining room was full of Americans who came with us. We had a small candlelit table.

The next day, Granny and Papa slept in while we went for a boat ride to a waterfall. We went with a group. When we arrived at the waterfall, a native calypso band was there. We danced and went under the calypso stick. We were young and it was fun to do. After that, we climbed the falls. Dunn River Falls in Jamaica. The natives called me a movie star. Upon climbing the falls, one of the tall and muscular natives picked me up and turned me upside down, and had me kiss John in that position. I was in excellent shape and young and had drunk a coco loco before the handstand on the river falls. The drink consisted of rum and coconut milk. It relaxed me. I did it as if I was a cheerleader. The group applauded and the photographer took our picture of the flip and kiss stand. We then climbed the falls. We went all the way to the top.

The next trip was Mexico City and Acapulco. Mexico City was big. We shopped in the downtown area where the buildings were tall and old. The shopping was good.

We bought some jewelry and clothing. The shoes I noticed were too small. The shoe sizes were 4, 5, and 6. The Mexican women had small feet. Many of the clothing items were too small for us.

We wined and dined in some of the finest hotels. One in particular I remember had violinists who played to us while we ate a fine dinner. We dressed in formal attire. John and I felt as if we were part of the royal family during the formal dinners in Mexico City.

We enjoyed Acapulco, also the water and the beaches. The motels were all on the beachfronts. We could hear the bands playing as we unpacked in our room. We toured the area we were staying at and did some shopping. We dealt with some men and young boys selling jewelry in the area.

The swimming pool was a large Roman design. It had cement walls around the pool. I felt like I was swimming in a Roman castle.

The weather was sunny and warm. We toured the highland and viewed some high divers dive off the high cliffs. Boaters hang-glided behind ski boats in Acapulco. We made many new friends on our trip to Mexico City and Acapulco and we took many pictures.

I started putting on some weight in my twenties. Mother was small, though even she had extra pounds at times, as I remember. Daddy was constantly dieting. I was at the age to wear pretty clothing and enjoy playing tennis and swimming. I visited my family doctor. Amphetamines (an upper) was the drug most widely used in those days. I remember when I took my first pill. I felt as if I was fifteen again. I could jog, run, play tennis, and clean my home without getting tired or hungry. Soon I became addicted to the amphetamines.

I joined a health spa and worked out. I looked as if I had stepped out of a James Bond movie. I began wearing clothing designed by Oscar D. Larenta, Bill Blass, and many others. Although the clothing was off the rack, it was beautiful and stylish. I enjoyed the feeling and life was glamorous for me -- traveling, being a young adult, winning art shows and being a member of the women's club. I felt as if I was on top of the world. I enjoyed being there for my daughter, listening to music on the radio. All my enjoyment was heightened.

After I lost weight, I became addicted to the feeling. I had a hard time sleeping at night, which called for a sleeping pill. It was time to stop the pills.

Slowly, I gained my weight back. At my family's insistence, I was admitted to a hospital to learn to deal with my weight and get off the medicine. I was given a mild antidepressant to deal with coming off the wonderful pill Melfiat.

We left the Chattanooga airport for the Bahamas, another island paradise. We again stayed in a motel on the beach. Guards, Bohemian guards, dressed in full uniform like the English, guarded the lobby. Standing in a posed still position, the guards were complete with hats and straps. After a rum punch party on the motel patio, we had a formal dinner banquet style, which all of our party attended. The food was good. Some of the fellow furniture dealers sitting with us planned a picnic on a deserted island near where we stayed. No one would be on our beachfront while we were occupied the beach area. One couple was from the Chattanooga area. The other couple was about our age.

The next morning, John and I got up and put our bathing suits on over our shorts. We wore sport shoes. The hotel prepared our lunch, which consisted of fruit, chicken, bread, and wine, all in a basket, enough for all six of us.

The island was small. After a time of getting to know one another, we ate the delicious lunch and drank the wine. After our meal we rubbed our bodies in oil and sunscreen and lay on our towels to soak up the sun. We rested about thirty minutes and then began exploring the water's edge. We swam under the water. The ocean's waves were mild on the island. We found some seashells and walked along the sandy beach. It was a relaxing feeling. Time passed quickly and too soon we heard the buzzing of the small boat approaching. The native came to pick us up. We boarded the boat after a relaxing day on the deserted island.

The few days in the Bahamas passed too soon. It was swimming, fine dining, rest, relaxing, and meeting new acquaintances. We enjoyed the trip at yet another island on the oceanfront.

John and myself are grandparents now. We live in Alabama still. Dad passed away in January of 2004. Cousin David Riggs also passed to the next life in May 2005. Both are buried in the Williams Cemetery along with Rudder Williams (the grandfather I never knew), Fronie, Analizbeth, Aunt Mae, Aunt Myrtle, Bettie Jo, John Denton, and Mrs. Riggs, David's mother, and many, many more relatives. Our daughter is now an attorney, a wife, and mother. John and I have two grandchildren: Melody, eight; and Stephen, six.

I want to give you a message from my heart. Parents, be good to your children. Listen to them and encourage them to attend college. Enjoy your family. Life is so precious.

There is so much child abuse in America. Our home surroundings and lifestyle affect us and our families.

Beginning In Business

The new furniture business was offered to us at the right time in our lives. John had long been interested in the furniture business. He had done clerical work for my father at the oil distributorship for several years after we were married. He left to open a small appliance and furniture store in our small town. John learned the business there. We won many trips to all places around the world selling appliances and televisions.

I was becoming tired of the beauty business. I was ready for a change in my life's work. I wanted to learn another line of work. I was not afraid of hard work, but I was tired of the constant gossip and long hours with little pay. I was thrilled about my husband being offered a new furniture business in a nearby Tennessee town. It had been there for several years and the owner decided to take some time off.

John and I left our professions and started to work in the new large furniture store. The store was laid out like a football field. We were pleased with its size. I walked down the store's aisle and viewed the furniture that occupied the store's floor.

Many sofas and chairs with tables and lamps lined the center aisles. The dining room suites were set up in the far right of the large building. Bedroom suites were lined up to the left of the store. The very front of the store contained many leader items, such as rockers, table lamps and curios. I was happy.

We met the staff employed by the first owner. The manager was a nice young family man. He was a Baptist preacher of a small congregation. A nice, sophisticated, proper-acting lady worked in the office. She was a grandmother and appreciated the job. She had been there for many years and knew the work well. There were three stock boys, a warehouse man, and two deliverymen. There were two salespeople, a man and a mature woman. Ron, the manager, filled in as a salesperson when we were busy. John decided I would fill in as a salesperson, which was fine with me -- I enjoyed working with families. When the customers came in for a purchase, they were pleasant to work with.

I soon forgot about the gossipy beauty shoppe. I waited on many families and obtained a large clientele. I also learned to do some of the office work. Every Thursday afternoon I worked in the office for Lona, the secretary. I took credit applications from the customers, which I also enjoyed. By working in the office I soon learned that almost all customers were approved. Most had lived in the same area for at least two years, had two credit references, and had been on the same job for at least two years.

I was also curious about the furniture we sold since the floor was full of furniture as well as many backups when we took over. I inquired about the furniture to Ron. He showed me the furniture lines up and down the aisles. We stopped at the bedroom section. Ron pulled out a drawer from the drawer chest. The suite was a 4065 Broyhill early American design in pine. We sold many, many suites in the group.

I asked him, "Why is this such a popular suite?"

"It's the right price," he said. "Look at the inside of the drawer."

He showed me the drawer pull. It was metal. The inside was mostly wood. It had good styling and the finish was also fine. It was well done, the price was right, and the quality was good. The dining room and living room suites were of good quality too. We sold name brand recliners also. We catered to young adults.

One day the May-Tag man came by to see if we wanted to sell their appliances. He talked with me; John was busy. He told me why the May-Tag man was almost never called for a repair. He also showed me how easily the washer was repaired when needed. The front of all May-Tags are easily taken off to replace any part that is needed. He also showed me how good the finish of a May-Tag is. He reached into his pocket and pulled out a quarter. He then took the quarter and tried to scratch some of the outside paint, but none came off. We decided to sell May-Tag.

We also needed a less expensive washer/dryer to offer the consumer, so we decided on Gibson. The Gibson held up well and had a good warranty. We could offer the washer for $100.00 less.

There we had it -- two good appliances to offer our customers. John was pleased. We sold the appliances and didn't have many problems with their service. We were pleased with both the furniture and the appliances we sold to the consumer.

Every morning we were at work by eight o'clock. We didn't open the doors until nine o'clock, which gave us time to go over what items to mark down for a quick sale.

We moved a lot of furniture in a month's time. We were the place to purchase some well-built and good design furniture for the best price.

We had to sell a lot of furniture to maintain the staff and cover the bills. We soon learned what to do to ensure a large profit by the end of the year. We advertised on television. After we had been in business for two years, we sent out flyers to the boxholders in our area. We sold to consumers within a 50-mile radius of the store.

All salespeople kept records as well as the company itself. The customers were sent special sale flyers to show them the large reduction in furniture items. We had special sales just for our customers. It was a good way to move items that didn't sell well due to high cost.

We decided to reduce the more expensive furniture items for the customers who had excellent credit. It was one way of moving the hard to sell furniture of excellent quality to the customers who patronized us.

Another way of insuring a sale in progress was to ask why they were hesitating on a living room suite for instance. If a customer sat on a sofa and wanted to purchase it, but hesitated for a while, we would ask the customers if they liked the group. If they replied affirmatively, we knew it was the cost that was keeping them from completing the sale. We sat down with them and offered them both lamps that were displayed with the group they were interested in for the price of only one. Then we gave them 90 days credit, the same as cash as well as free set up and delivery within 50 miles. This was not a great reduction for us, however, we wanted to move a large amount and make the customer happy, which meant repeat customers.

If a customer sat at a group for a long time and didn't buy, we would have lost the sale if they shopped somewhere else. We had to think of everything in order to keep the business profitable. We wanted to be successful in business five years down the road. We had to pay off our new furniture incoming bills as well as the help and overhead.

We learned which mattresses to sell. We didn't want any problems with any of our merchandise. Certain mattresses had warranties. Some were foam, some were coil springs, and some were water mattresses. We sold them all. We sold the inexpensive waterbed mattresses complete with heater. We sold a better waterbed mattress that had a foundation with it like the regular mattress. We sold foam mattresses complete with springs. We also sold bunkies complete with boards. We didn't want problems with them, so we sold the best. We had cutaways to show the customer how the mattresses were constructed. The heaviest gauge coil springs lasted the longest. Although it cost a little ore, it was worth it. They held up better and almost all mattresses lasted out their warranties.

We strove to be the store that had it all. Whatever the customer wanted for their home, we had it from bunk beds to bedroom groups to sofas and love seats to recliners to rockers to mattresses to bunkies to waterbeds to appliances and curios, occasional tables and coffee tables. We had it all at our furniture store. We had backups in all the furniture groups too. When we sold one group, we backed it up with the one just like it in the warehouse.

We were also not undersold by anyone in a 50-mile radius. We hired more help and after a year increased the help's paycheck by one and a half percent. We took out some health insurance and gave about a five percentage to each salesperson for each sale item they sold. This gave the salespeople an incentive to sell more.

As our inventory left the floor and when we ran out of backup inventory, we simply called the sales rep and reordered the group what we were out of. This went on until we ran out of all our inventory once.

In January of every year we went to Atlanta for the furniture market. We visited every floor for viewing the furniture there. We took a bank statement from our banker to show we had credit to purchase the vendor's merchandise. Later we used Dunn and Bradstreet. However, we had to build up to that credit rating. Upon entering each space, we were met by a sales rep for our area. We signed in and then were shown the furniture. The sales rep for our area informed us of what was fast-moving in the other stores. We always took their advice for our purchases. We ordered in January and by spring we received all the new merchandise. We would order at least four of each suite for backups.

Every January we attended the Atlanta Furniture Market in the big, high building in downtown Atlanta. Upon entering the market, we filled out nametags, business credits, our location, and so forth. A business reference was kept on file for years to come for the vendors and representatives of each market space.

We wore our nametags to the different vendor spaces. Vendor means manufacturers of the furniture brands. We knew what price range to buy for in our area. We catered to the young adult market. That was where the money was. Young adults who were getting married need a lot of furniture. They purchased bedrooms, bedding, living room suites -- a full house purchase.

My first large sale was to a couple. They purchased $10,000 in furniture needs and appliances as well. We sold frames for beds and mattresses. We sold beautiful lamps of all types.

All the furniture was lined up back to back for a quick sale. For instance, a sofa and love seat with matching tables and lamps, or dining room groups, or bedroom groups complete with a mattress setup. However, we did not add the mattress to the set group price. Sometimes the customer had a mattress and did not purchase one. We tried to keep the price down for the customer.

We shopped the bottom of the markets' huge buildings for the bargains. We purchased furniture that was not well known. We checked out the quality of the goods in order to keep the price low enough to keep the business going well. We wanted to make a lot of money and offer a good product to the consumer. That took a lot of work on our part. In other words, we had to check the quality of all the furniture goods we purchased.

We slowly worked our way up with vendors such as Broyhill and Clanton Marcus. We knew it was well made and they would back it up. We learned to purchase the deals as well as the market specials. Sometimes if you purchased the entire floor of the market specials, it was at a record low price. Such a deal ensured us a beautiful floor of a top vendor. We made money as well as dressed up our floor. By attending market, we were able to have quality priced furniture for a very reasonable price. We had an overhead to cover as well as purchase furniture and make payroll. We did, and still made a profit and enjoyed the work. It was the best life I ever had. Champagne was always served in our room at market, as well as fruit. We ate at the best restaurants in Atlanta.

We made friends with the vendors' reps. They gave us their business cards with the home and business phone numbers. We kept them on file for reference. If we needed any merchandise, we could contact them at once. Delivery of a new furniture order was about three to six weeks depending on the cutting of the particular suite we were ordering.

We could depend on the sales rep for service. When a rep comes into the store, it's best to stop what you're doing and take him or her to your office. There you can order what you need in private. They can also inform you of the new cuttings available for the next shipment. They will give you books on all new suites. However, we tried to keep the latest furniture groups in upholstery and all furniture items.

We advertised with leader items. Furniture items such as curios, lamps, five-drawer chests, full beds, mattresses, recliners, ottomans, wooden rockers, and hall trees. We simply purchased a lot of leader items at a reduction in price. Sell them close to wholesale price in order to get the clientele in the store to purchase the big furniture items. A leader item sale is usually in January and February when traffic is low. These sales help move furniture in the slow months.

Also when a freelance lamp salesperson comes to your store with a truckload of lamps or furniture from an unknown furniture factory, talk to them in your office. Ask about the quality. Go out to the truck and check out the quality of the merchandise yourself. Check to see if the furniture is hardwood and also if it's put together well. The lamps also.

These items can be sold for more than half what they usually sell for because they're not well known. However, if you check them out yourself, and the paint is applied well to the stylish lamp and the lamps are in the latest colors, as well as neutrals, then you have done the work yourself. Take a bow and make yourself some money by marking up the price.

Another way to pick up traffic in the store is to make some TV commercials. I was asked by my husband and our manager to do some TV spots for the store. I walked the aisles of the store to view the many furniture items for sale. I wrote down every furniture piece that was on sale, including the best leader items. Many of the furniture items sold for less than in the metropolitan areas.

We sold good quality furniture for a reduced price. We also mapped the area within a 50-mile radius. We decided to deliver furniture free within that radius, which increased our business. After a meeting with my husband and the manager, I was off to the television station to do a commercial. I was met by the sales rep from the station. He became a friend of ours. Dale Meader was a singer and also a sales rep for the company. He sat me down in front of the camera for the spot.

"Jan," he said, "it will be a thirty-second spot."

The tall, handsome, soft-spoken Dale Meader told me to look into the camera while making the commercial. I did and one take was made.

"Okay," said Dale. "We need to make another one or two. Now," he said, "talk a little slower and drop your diction. Just do it without your southern talk."

I did and the third one was a take for the commercial. We went back into the viewing room to see the spot we had just made. It was excellent. The lighting was good.I wore a blue suit. We had many sales after that spot. John was pleased and so was our staff. We gained new business and the salespeople earned more money as well as us making a profit.

Ordinarily, a paper ad is all that's needed to bring in sales. However, it was the two slowest months of the year, January and February, we had to spend money to make money. The rest of the year we sent out flyers to each boxholder. This was an advertisement that had all the leader items and special upholstery on sale. Sometimes we did a commercial called a jingle for the radio in our area. It worked well. We also had special sales for our approved credit customers.

One day we hired more help as our business increased and we needed more help. Milan was introduced to me by Ron, our manager. He was an intelligent man. He was also kind and a family man. He knew the furniture business. He taught me a lot and we became friends. Milan was an asset to the company. We had some lamp breakage on deliveries. He showed the deliverymen how to load the furniture for low damage. As he wrapped a few lamps with cushion and packed them in boxes, I watched the delivermen wrap the sofas in paper and lay a lot of cushion foam paper down on the bed of the truck. Less damage kept the cost down and saved time. This insured the customer being happy with their merchandise.

As a result of low damage and the pickup in the clientele, we increased our profits. Milan had earned his salary. He was an asset to our business. We all learned to appreciate his efforts.

We learned that beginning in business and becoming a success is like a cake recipe. If you have the right ingredients to make the cake, then bake the cake according to specifications, it will turn out well.

Recipe for having a successful furniture business. Throw in a dash of knowing you product. Sprinkle with a few sales staff that have a lot in common and enjoy working with people. Add to your knowledge and learn what style furniture sells in your area. Whip in some advertising during the slow months. Put on the icing by keeping the sales floor attractive. Don't forget to add a dash of small leader items for the sales floor.

We did all of these things and tasted the joy of success in business. We will always remember the wonderful years that we were in the furniture business.

Janice and her family eating at Grammy's on a Holiday.

Decorating Advice

I have worked in exclusive furniture sales for many years. I have attended many decorator workshops. I am a world traveler. I am also an artist, a poet, a writer, and a decorator.

Decorating is simple if you know what type of furniture to use for your style of home.

Now, eclectic grouping of the three styles of furniture is used as well as antiques. For instance, if your husband insists on using a contemporary sectional, you can use your antique given to you by your aunt if you wish to; it's okay.

If your home is a colonial brick with columns, chances are you prefer traditional furniture mixed with some antiques and early American. Coffee tables made of mahogany wood or maple wood with a rose wood trim and Queen Ann legs are an excellent choice. However, they are very expensive.

We have a flea market sales at First Monday near where we live. All types of furniture are displayed at First Monday every month in Scottsboro, Alabama, at low flea market prices. The sale of the home merchandise is displayed all around the square in nearby Scottsboro, Alabama.

Sometimes used furniture in good condition can set off your room decor and make your room full of furniture look more elegant and exquisite.

It is a good idea to purchase an antique value book. This will enable you to know the value of the purchase you make, whether it is an antique, a dish, or a furniture item.

When purchasing occasional tables for your home, it is more stylish to have three different shapes, such as a round, a square, or an oval or a butler's tray octagonal table.

Oriental rugs are fashionable for a dressy "up town look." They can be used even over a low pile carpet. This gives the room charm and adds warmth.

Wing chairs are necessary for the elegant dressy look.

A ball and claw foot secretary in mahogany would make the room have more atmosphere in a traditional living room; it would add character. Mahogany is a dark wood usually found on most ball and claw secretaries. My grandmother left one to my daughter. The antique adds a lot to the room. It is priceless to her.

If you purchase one on the open market, the cost is usually three to four thousand dollars. Again, if you can find a used one at a flea market, buy it quickly. It is an excellent buy for the living room. If you were fortunate enough to be left any cherry dining room occasional tables or Chippendale chairs in mahogany, cherish them. They make good additions to your home and help give your decor character.

I was asked to help pick out some paint trim for my parents' summer home on the lake soon after I became a decorator. The home had a new roof already installed. The home was of gray rock. The roof was a medium brown. The color was not a good combination. It did not look as though the roof went with the house. Dad had purchased a bargain

on the roofing material.

The wooden doors were dressy hand-carved wood in squares. The door pulls were pewter.

I remembered in one of my workshops that a home on the lake or sea front should be a loud, festive color. I could have chosen a turquoise blue. I could have chosen a river green. I could have painted the door a mud color. However, I decided to go with a mauve and paint the doors a slate color because the roof lines were sheik, and the home was in a high-income area. The home was valued at three hundred thousand dollars.

The painters were shocked at the color. However, at my insistence, they began to paint. The mauve brought together the mismatched brown roof and gray rock. It brightened the home up. The doors of slate were lightened up a bit. The door pulls were left a pewter. The home was beautiful and looked what it was worth.

Color is important to the interior of the home as well as on the outside of the home. My many courses in color and trips to many countries helped me in choosing the right color.

You can gage color sometimes by your clothing. For instance, if you wear a navy dress, you might brighten up the color up with red accessories. All that you know comes in handy when it comes to color coordinating. Sometimes three lights and darks of one color bring out the wood, such as dark mauve, medium mauve, and light mauve.

The wood carved door on my dad's lake house could have been in three colors of mauve to show up the woodwork on the door. However, I decided not to do that. The reason was that the house was of a gray rock, and it was cut to look like a long brick. The roofline was long. The home was contemporary in design. It had a lot of class. The home was sheik.

It had a swimming pool as large as the Holiday Inn's. There was enough wood trim on the house to paint the mauve color, including the private wooden fence that partly surrounded the pool area. The house brought top dollar after a good clean up and a trim paint job of a bright festive color.

After you've decided what colors to use for your home, it's good to draw your rooms off on scale paper before you shop for furniture. First, you need to purchase some scale paper at the store. Each square represents twelve inches. Take a tape measure with you when you go shopping. Also a slide rule is good to have when measuring your floors. The length of the room and the width of the room are what you need. Then draw it off to scale onto the paper. This is much needed so that you can make sure the furniture is spaced far enough apart so you can walk around the room freely with out bumping into it.

Also your furniture needs to be balanced in a room. For instance, if you have a sofa on one side of the room, then perhaps two wing back chairs spaced a little apart for a table and lamp will balance the sofa. This way when some are sitting on the sofa, some guests will sit in the wing chairs. You have to balance the room for good decorating. The chairs don't have to be wing backs; they can be any design you want.

Also the focal point of the room such as a fireplace mantel has to have balance. You need to have the larger piece, such as a mirror, taller in the center and maybe a big vase a little smaller and not as tall by each side of the mirror. Then, if you have room on the hearth, some candles a little shorter on either end of the mantel are nice. This would be a line elevating up on each side to a point in the center. It is balanced. It's easy to do.

If you have a wall facing the fireplace and have room, you may want to put in a narrow console curio and hang a painting over it. This would balance the opposite side of the fireplace. It's all about walkways, balance, and color.

The fabric you choose as well means a lot. If you want to use the room frequently, you might want to use durable fabric. A sales person is qualified to assist you in this case. Freely ask her or him any question about the fabric for your furniture, sofa, and chair purchases.

Accents to a room and accessories are a good mixture to have in your room decor. For instance, a ficus tree set in the corner of the room is all the go now. Also candles set on a cocktail table, the fireplace mantel, and the dining room table are very popular.

If you entertain for a special event such as a wedding, fresh roses or some fresh flowers set in a silver container are called for. However, when you're not entertaining, sometimes silk flowers are a nice arrangement to have. Aside from silk flowers, real plants of many different kinds of greenery such as ferns and elephant ears scattered throughout the home are a nice touch.

Accessories of many types to accent your decor are in demand for the decorated home. For early American decor, eagles, pilgrims, and baskets of daisies in pictures hung on the walls enhance the early American decor. I saw a painting of a rocker with an afghan folded and placed on the back of the ladder-back rocker. I remember the artist, Hubert Suptrine. I also saw a bucket of apples under a faucet with water running over the bucket and apples. Roosters, ducks, etc., are wonderful complements to the country or early American decor.

Also big poster beds are excellent to use for a country villa or in a farm house with a front porch all the way around the house. Braided rugs are a must for a country look, as are antique headboards, spindle headboards, foot boards, and spindle chairs with early American tables with spindle legs. Spinning wheels, horses, and cows in paintings are also attractive. Just go country all the way when you decorate the farmhouse and the log houses, or if you just simply like the early American country look.

Decorating the old fifty's downstairs level was also interesting. The size of the downstairs made me think of a ship. The living area was paneled with a maple wood. The fireplace was made of old brick. The brick had been taken from an old burned building. The color of the brick was mauve, silver, and slate. There was a maple wood mantel and an opening at the end of the hearth for a small TV. The kitchen was long, and the appliances were built in. There was a place under the stairs for a small refrigerator. Near the sink on the left side was a small opening for a built-in refrigerator. Two Dutch ovens occupied a space in this kitchen. It was neat. The cabinets were maple with indirect lighting over the cabinets.

There was one master bedroom with double closets, a huge window, and a space for a TV on the opposite wall of the bed. Down the hall were three bedrooms, one small bedroom and two a little larger. A linen closet was at the end of the hall.

The whole downstairs was paneled with maple paneling.

I started in the kitchen. I painted the cabinets a maple color. I had new almond appliances installed in their spaces. I had the carpet pulled up in the living space, and I had the wooden floors painted a high gloss of maple color on the floors to look as if it were on a ship. I put down a braided rug and added a plaid sofa with some beige, mauve, and brown colors.

I put two leather chairs and ottomans opposite the Sofa. Wooden lamps were put on two small lamp tables beside the sofa. A large wall clock hung on the opposite wall. I put a round table in a small place in the end of the kitchen. I placed a small candleholder on a tablecloth on the table. On a piece of board, I mounted a bell at the bottom of the stairs along with a ship's steering wheel.

In the large bedroom I had a large headboard made for a wall mount covered in a beige nubby fabric to simulate a suite on a ship. Two wall lights were mounted on the wall above two pieces of wood for a nightstand. I used a small dresser and a small mirror mounted on the wall above the small dresser.

In the back room, I had the walls painted in a sky blue with sea gulls flying in the clouds. On the bottom half of the room's walls, I had an artist paint the wall to look like the inside of a ship, complete with life jackets and life preservers, along with small boats painted on. Then I had a whirlpool installed.

The downstairs was complete. It made me feel as though I was on a ship -- the high gloss floors, the round porthole, simulated windows with a sea picture inside the round window frames. It was now not only a downstairs level, but also an escape from one's daily routine.

The upstairs was done in a ritzy New York apartment look. Everyone was pleased with the decor on the two levels.

You can make a name for yourself if you're a designer by simply using the theme decorating idea. Also you might ask the homeowners to recommend you to a client if they like your home decor. Word of mouth is the best way to get your name out there.

When you've had decorator training and have worked in decorating many homes, upon entering a room that needs decorating, you can get a mental picture of what the room would look like if you decorated it. For instance, my husband and I went to see his aunt in Arlington, Virginia, the other day.

I went downstairs for something for her and became astonished at the possibilities of the room being decorated as if it were a VP waiting room in an airport. I could envision the posts having boards with arrows painted on them in different directions, and I envisioned a purple indoor-outdoor carpet on the floor. I could imagine small pictures on the windows and on the walls posters of airplanes. There could be added small metal chairs that could probably be purchased from an office supply or a doctor's waiting room that is being moved to another location. I would have wall mounts for small televisions and a wet bar and some stools.

There was also a bathroom down there. I could paint a woman's and a man's outline on the door. I could see some round tables with chairs and some twin-sized beds up against the walls with bolster pillows with some room dividers for privacy.

I saw all this in my mind before going back upstairs at my husband's aunt's. You just do that when you are a decorator. It could be done easily.

Fabrics are important in the durability of your new sofa ensemble. Cotton and polyester blends in a number of prints are widely used on the casual sofas. Polished cotton blends and a velvet look are used for formal living areas: red violet and red, red orange, orange, yellow orange, yellow green, green, blue green, blue violet.

The three secondary colors orange, violet, and green are made by mixing equal parts of two primary colors. At this point, fasten your seat belts because you're headed for a color eruption. By mixing the primary and secondary colors, you will come up with six intermediate or tertiary colors. Tint a hue lighter by adding white; shade it darker by black; dull its intensity by adding gray.

There are several ways to build a color scheme by playing with the color wheel. A monochromatic scheme is based on tints and shades of a single color because their color variation (black, white, and neutrals don't count) texture becomes important in order to avoid monotony.

Like a colored plaid joined with chairs of a nonshiny and woven texture, an analogous color scheme makes use of colors used side by side on the color wheel.

You'll use these base-related, like yellow, yellow-green, and green, interesting and refreshing because of the change of pace in intensity and value.

A complimentary scheme is based on using colors that are opposite the color wheel, like blue and orange, or red and green. They create a sharp, decisive look, particularly suitable for contemporary rooms. Be sure that one color leads, with the others as accents.

I take my colors out of the fabric or a rug, or a painting. For instance if you use a plaid fabric - take a sold color out of the plaid fabric for a chair, and use a solid Love seat - add pillows of a plain color from the plaid sofa, or plaid pillows mixed with the plain color from the sofa fabric. Add a rug with the colors in the sofa and a framed print of the same colors for the wall.

If the outside of your home is a smooth line contemporary design, then chances are you prefer contemporary design furniture. Think pieces all the way –- cubes, circles, and squares. These are the shapes of the cocktail and accessory tables to be used.

Glass square tables with plain square sectionals are usually called for in the contemporary decor. In the bedroom a contemporary wall bed with a lighted headboard is nice. A modern statue in a spacious living area is a pretty accent piece to use. It is a nice conversation piece to add to your contemporary home decor.

I like to think of a high-rise apartment when I think contemporary. Just imagine an Oriental white sofa with square accent tables in mahogany mixed with some Oriental Chippendale chairs and an off-white Oriental rug with a pole light for extra soft light and a modern design painting over the sofa or the fireplace.

Do you get the picture? Yes, Oriental Chippendale can be used with contemporary easily. It gives the room an uptown look. Modern glass candlestick holders and pastel candles give the room a romantic warm feeling. This is called putting on the Ritz.

Of course, you don't have to spend a fortune. Cover a square frame sofa with a silk blend white fabric with an imprint design. Use a flea market find of contemporary oak and glass square cocktail table with matching end tables, and there you have it, a swanky uptown look. Bring out the candles; purchase a flea market find of plain candleholders, and the room will look as though you spent a small fortune.

It's the room as a whole that comes together that makes a professional look. Comments on a room well done should be "I love the room." "Everything in this room is well coordinated." "I just don't know what piece of furniture it is that makes this room look great."

In other words, try not to have a single piece of furniture stand out. Try not to have a star piece unless you have a magnificent piece you want as your focal point.

If you have a fancy mirror that overpowers the fireplace mantel and that is a magnificent antique, then go ahead and do it. The company you invited will talk about it. Their eye will go directly to the oversized mirror. And, you will have successfully shown off the prize piece.

Pink light bulbs can be purchased to give the room a more complimentary lighting effect. Decorators often suggest pink lighting.

Although lace curtains were used in the eighteenth century for draperies, they are still good today. The curtain rod should be hung eight inches above the curtain window. A three-inch width hem allowance should be on each side of the curtain. Also an eight-inch hem allowance is correct at the hem of your curtain.

My parents always had a decorator make their curtains. I noticed how well they were made as a child. There were even small weights at the edge and center of their curtains. This was to hold the curtain in the correct place and keep the hemline down where it belonged.

Today, window treatments are widely used. A curtain valance with a blind is widely used. However, I prefer a curtain rod that accents the type of period furniture I use.

For instance, when using a mixture of Queen Anne and traditional and French together, a wooden fancy curtain rod is good to use. Polished cotton with a flat rod of sheers of white and tie backs are flattering to use in such a décor, and so are lace curtains. A curtain is needed when you want privacy. If your home is far off the highway and no one can see in your windows, try not using curtains. The sunlight and the feeling of being out in nature are good to have in your home atmosphere.

Wooden curtain valances are out of date. However, some decorators use them in children's rooms all the way across for special decorating, such as displaying a nursery rhyme like "Peter Cottontail." It could be written onto the wooden curtain valance.

In special rooms the decorator uses whatever is called for. In a stately room of a silk blend material, a cloth valance is better than a wooden one. I prefer just a plain curtain of good material with no valance.

A traditional design of furniture is best for the colonial brick home with columns. It is a blend of Chippendale, Queen Anne, Hepple white, and French in design. You may find this combination in most all home magazines. The White House and all heads of state such as governors use this combination of design of furniture. It is also widely used by the wealthy. Rose wood, mahogany wood, cherry wood, and maple wood are mostly used in the stately design furniture. They are your best hard woods.

The movie *Father of the Bride* and the TV sitcom with Michael J. Fox as a senator display the stately furniture. If you rent the movies *Sleeping with Enemy* and *Father of the Bride,* run back over the movies slowly.

For instance, in *Sleeping with the Enemy, w*hen the star leaves the enemy, her husband, she leaves a contemporary designed home on the ocean front and goes to a farmhouse with a big front porch -- a complete opposite from the modular design furniture in the contemporary oceanfront home. The farmhouse is completely country in design and is a mixture of antique beds, ruffle skirt chairs, and draperies. The kitchen is country as well.

However, in *Father of the Bride* the stately design furniture look was used throughout the home. The color scheme was excellent also. The dining room table used was a cherry wood along with Queen Anne chairs. The furniture in *Father of the Bride* was a classic mixture of traditional, Queen Anne, and French.

After viewing these films, you will have a better understanding of what design furniture mixture you most want for your home.

Also Oriental furniture such as black lacquer goes well with any plain line of furniture. Sometimes a dining room of Oriental design is chosen, although the living room is a mixture of furniture. However, it is a good idea to use plain straight lines of furniture when mixing Oriental with your décor -- again, modern mixed with Oriental.

The shutters and colonial home with columns are best for the traditional design furniture and stately mixture.

The old colonial homes are better decorated in a classic way. In other words use authentic accent pieces. You may want to check out of the library a history of George Washington or maybe Louie the 14th and 15th. You could use traditional and early American furniture with Queen Anne accessories and some blends of antiques. You might want to go with strictly early American. An idea for the dining room, purchase an American flag. Either purchase plain white wallpaper and also red wallpaper or maroon wallpaper. Now, with a measuring stick, draw wide lines for the white wallpaper and smaller ones for the red or maroon wallpaper. Then cut the paper to fit the lines. If this wall treatment seems too time-consuming, you might want to purchase some striped wallpaper in shades of white and red or maroon. The look you want is a patriotic look. A nice touch for window treatment is white balloon curtains with gold stars sewn on them. Also blue or red curtains would be an excellent choice. Just the plain draw drapes. A cherry or mahogany dining room suite is nice if you prefer a dark wood early American dining room group.

If the dining room is a dressy one with a cherry or mahogany dining room suite that is in a high varnish, then use fine china and purchase a picture in a dark frame of George and Martha Washington. Old poster beds are called for in the bedrooms and also lace curtains with wooden rods are what they used a century ago. It's authentic decorating. An antique sofa with a rose carved on the back of the sofa is a nice added feature. They have reproductions of these antiques. Look for antique reproductions for your old historical homes. They compliment the period of the home.

The foyer of the home is usually decked with a hall tree and an umbrella stand along with some ferns on a plant stand. Wing chairs are usually put by the fireplace. The kitchens are usually out of date; however, add an island for a workspace. These kitchens are, as a rule, very large. Have indirect lighting put in; put in some stained glass windows for your windows to add atmosphere and privacy.

When you have decorated to perfection and you don't live in the home long, you will create a high selling price for your home and furniture. The home will be marvelously attractive and in the correct decor for the period. You can make some money on the home in the resale market.

Theme decorating is all the go now. You can make a room look any way you want and have any type feel. For instance, if you want a feeling of floating on a cloud in a bedroom, just paint the room light blue, and then paint white clouds all around the walls. Use light, off-white carpet. A Hollywood bed frame in king size is widely used for comfort. You will have the feeling of floating on a cloud. It's a calm feeling, and the stress of the day will disappear. You will most probably sleep well.

If you like the outside and camping, how do you like the idea of a waterfall mural in your bedroom? Put the mural up on the bedroom walls. Use grass green or gray rock color carpet and slide a queen-sized bed frame up against the water fall mural. Use a green and light brown and amber leaf print spread and drapes. You will feel as though you're outside. You will feel serene if you love camping. If you want to, you can even paint tiny, silver stars on the ceiling of your bedroom.

Go ahead and try your fantasy. It's your home and your dream of what is a good feeling for you.

My husband and I decided to purchase a hot tub. We had a room downstairs we did not use. It had no windows. I decided to put up some wallpaper to make it feel as though we were in the jungle. I got the idea when we were in Hawaii. There was jungle wallpaper in the hotel where we stayed.

I told the lady at the wallpaper store about the wallpaper. She checked into it, and I ordered the wallpaper. I had the wallpaper put on the walls. I purchased a large hot tub and had it installed in the room. I also purchased a tape of the sounds of nature in the jungle at the store. We feel so relaxed when we use our hot tub. We sleep well after sitting in our jungle hot tub in our room.

If your home is a French Tudor design, then the fireplace should display an iron pot and a pot holder. An early American dark pine open China table with hutch is probably your best choice for the dining area. However, you might be able to find an old antique mahogany Jacobean table and chairs. An early American oak wash table is also correct, as well as a spindle back chairs. Shaker furniture is good to use as well. However, I prefer the big early American look or the Jacobean furniture.

In the living room, country French or early American furniture is called for. A hickory chair makes an excellent coup-French group complete with wide French chairs with a cotton blend fabric with a ruffle at the bottom of the chairs and sofas. Big poster beds are in order for the many bedrooms. Rice carved beds and armoires are good to use in the large bedrooms. These homes have a lot of atmosphere. They make you think of being in the English countryside. These homes are best placed on several-acre areas of land.

In a log home, simple, simple is the decor. You may use old wooden tables. I have an idea. Say you found an old farm house Shaker table at the flea market. Just take a chain and swing it over your left arm and let it fall easily over the old table, hitting the table lightly from end to end, three inches apart until you have covered the entire table. It is not necessary to do the legs of the table; they might be damaged in the process. However, if you feel you must have the distressed look on the table, hold the chair in your hand about one inch from the leg. Lightly tap the leg all over for a distressed look, but remember to be careful not to damage the furniture piece.

After you have completed the "destressing" of the old table, go to the art shop and purchase some antiquing kits, or paint the table a Williamsburg blue: a blue gray.

Braided rugs are called for. Kerosene lamps are a nice light for the homes. Homemade quilts are good to use on the beds. Remember, the more rustic the furniture, the better.

Wood groups in pine with cushions are an excellent choice. The fabrics come in a nylon with daisies or an old spinning wheel fabric pattern. I think they're made in Athens, Tennessee. You might find one at a flea market. Country plates and jars for drinking glasses are excellent authentic choices for the old log homes.

Decorating problems in the home can be corrected. For instance, a dining room with no room for much furniture you could add a narrow library table. That might help with the lack of space in the room. Also two small china hutches built in may help.

When I was a teen, I remember my mother having a decorator. She decorated a small porch area of the home into a dining room for our summer home, which we sometimes used for a winter retreat.

The decorator, at Mom's request, held down the cost of the decor. She found a narrow Spanish design table with strong black leather Spanish chairs. The decorator had a cabinetmaker build in two cabinets on each end of the room for some dishes and some accessories. The cabinets were all the way to the floor. Wine carpet was used. She painted the cabinets a celery color to blend with the colors in the other part of the house. These were colors opposite the color wheels. However, they complement well.

To carry out the color selection, the decorator used two wine chairs and a Spanish table in the foyer overlooking the pool area. The master bedroom was the next room after entering the foyer. There the walls were again celery in color. The colors blended well with the dining room. Mauve carpet would be used today instead of the wine. Also, taupe and neutral carpets are widely used today. And bright colors are used on the walls.

I had a decorating problem in my kitchen. We had old pine cabinets. John, my husband, wanted to keep the cabinets. I didn't argue with him. I had old cabinets, but they were in good condition. They were painted in a clear varnish to dress them up. I then chose a bright floral wallpaper of blue, orange, and pink. I also purchased wallpaper that had fabric that matched the floral print.

I had a curtain valance of the same fabric put up and added a small tassel trim. The draperies were draw drapes. The tablecloth for the round table was in a plaid of the same colors as the wallpaper.

The place setting was of a china in a coordinating color. The glasses were pink. When I had guests over for a small dinner, they commented on how beautiful the kitchen was. "This is a doll kitchen." "This is the prettiest room in the house." No one ever noticed the out-of-date cabinets.

A Problem Solved, the Remodeling of an Old Historical Home Kitchen:

The old home was in excellent condition for sale, except for the kitchen. As I entered the kitchen, I could see that it was too dark and needed to be lighted with some recessed lights overhead. I decided to paint the cabinets a medium blue. I picked out some beige, blue and yellow daisy flower wallpaper. This gave the kitchen a country look and lightened it up. On the floor, I decided to use a square tile of yellow and beige. I then added an island for more workspace.

With the new wallpaper, cabinets painted and new tile and island, I decided to add some almond appliances. This brought the old kitchen up to date as well as brightening up the dark old kitchen.

I could have painted the kitchen a sunlight yellow. I could have used squares of yellow and white tile on the floor. I also could have used a dark rich brown color on the cabinets. This also would have lightened up the kitchen.

Decorate a room in your home to give you the feeling you're on an island -- or perhaps a waiting room in an airport. Use the African influence or just use your imagination. For instance, what is your favorite place? After you decide, then decorate accordingly. Make your home an escape from your daily routine, or just make it tastefully decorated and comfortable. You're in command of your own space in your abode.

My daughter and son-in-law just purchased a new home. It is simply beautiful. The ceilings are high, and there are many rooms. Just as you come into the foyer of the home, there are high ceilings and a large wall space to decorate in front of the staircase. The dining room is to the left of the foyer just as you enter the home. The furniture is French and off white in color.

Renoir, pronounced "ren-wah," was a French impressionist artist, one of the old masters. He painted events such as picnics, boat rides, and ladies and gentleman in fancy attire. He caught French girls in ballet, in fancy hats, and in many more dressy events.

I had a brainstorm about decorating the high walls in the foyer of my daughter's home.

She had a beautiful wedding, and all the bridesmaids were young and beautiful. The photographer caught them on film in the room just before the wedding. The dresses were dark peach. The bridesmaids had fancy floral bands in their hair. My daughter had on a beautiful white wedding gown with a lot of beesa with a pearl necklace also. We decided to have that picture blown up to a very large one; we touched it up to show off the pretty young faces of the bridesmaids and the bride. It was beautiful.

The frame chosen was a gold baroque. The picture resembles a Renoir pose. It is a unique idea for a large wall space.

The next thing to master is the theme in decorating your main home or your summer home. Our home, for instance, is a traditional brick. The front is decorated by an early American curvy wood frame and early American columns. The back of the home has solid glass across the whole back of the house. I could have gone traditional or contemporary; either one would have been correct.

It was time to redo our home. We removed all the old furniture. We also removed the old draperies. In the living room were some velvet draperies. I had a glass chandelier. It was a formal look. I took a good look at the room after the furniture was removed and the velvet draperies. I did not want the room to be very formal again. However, I did want a dressy look.

I stood back in the living room and noticed how beautiful the cathedral ceiling looked. The fireplace had a beautiful hearth, and the whole wall was covered in mountain pastel rock. There was also a mantel made out of the rock. The floor was squares of wood. One side of the room was solid glass sliding doors. A terrace was just outside the window.

After cleaning the room thoroughly, I decided to decorate, picking up the colors from the mountain rock of the focal point -- the fireplace. I purchased a thick-pillowed, light off-white sofa and love settee. The pillows were the colors in the rock: mauve, light blue, and pinkish beige. I decided upon using an Oriental rug in front of the sofa of pastel colors. I chose a small round cocktail table of maple trim wood and a square and oval end table. An antique brass chandelier I chose to hang just below the maple colored cathedral ceiling.

Draperies were not needed since we were so far off the road from the back. However, I chose a polished cotton of off white to match the sofa. A dull brass curtain rod and curtains were chosen to hold the plain draperies for this room. The draperies were only used for when the sun was brightly shining into the room and at night.

Pillows of mauve were used on the hearth for seating for special occasions. The room was dressy without being overpoweringly formal. It was a pleasant experience sitting in the room after the decorating changeover.

How to purchase furniture and items for your home:

Be sure all the furniture you purchase fits the room. Don't overpower the room with furniture. You want to be able to walk around the room without bumping into any piece of furniture. Most bedrooms are too small for a king-sized bed. However, if you must have one, leave off the nightstand and hang up two wall lights on either side of your bed for lighting. You might want to leave off a dresser and have two small chests. Just remember to allow for enough space for your furniture.

If you're planning on purchasing a comfortable chair for the den, Recliners are widely chosen and are a good choice.

However, a nice, more dressy chair is the leather chair and ottoman. They're better looking and very comfortable. The in colors and type fabric chosen for the chairs and ottomans is leather; the colors are oxblood, navy, blue, and neutral, as in various shades of beige. Almost always decorators prefer a leather chair and ottoman instead of the widely used recliner.

Accents to a room and accessories are a good mixture to have with your room decor. Candles on the coffee table, the fireplace mantel, and the dining room table are also popular. A centerpiece on a table in the dining room is nice to have.

Aside from silk flowers, a real plant of many kinds of greenery is in style throughout the living area and in the foyer. Accessories of many kinds help make the decor complete, for instance, eagles, brass, and pictures of pilgrims and baskets with daisies in paintings.

For instance, I saw a painting of an old rocking chair with an afghan folded over the back. I remember the name of the artist; it was Hubert Subtrine. Prints of the rocker-afghan wouldn't be very expensive to purchase if you like the early American look, sometimes called a country look. Any accessory or painting would work, for instance a painting of wood and daises or a bucket of apples under a faucet. Baskets, pewter, and pictures of an old barn or roosters, ducks, etc. Get the idea of what to use for your accessories if you want a country look?

In one of my many workshop classes, I learned about a technique called a waxed fruit effect on the walls. This technique works so well with velvet curtains and silk sofas and chairs. Glass chandeliers would be an excellent choice also with the high gloss walls.

I purchased some aborigine pain and also some medium apricot color interior wall paint. I painted the walls with some of each color paint to see the effect of the colors with the high gloss over it. It was beautiful and elegant, very unique. It did look like waxed fruit. This is a new idea to use when painting sheet rock walls for an elegant look.

I helped in decorating one of my friend's children's rooms. I decided to paint the walls an ocean blue. I painted them a medium blue, turquoise, and dark blue. I drew a large circle on the ceiling with points all around it. I then painted the circle and points orange to represent the sun. I then painted some different colors of green on the walls for seaweed. Then I painted some fish on the wall of orange, yellow, and gold. I got creative and painted some bubbles coming up from a child swimming with goggles on, on the wall. It appeared as if the child was swimming underwater with the fish. I found a headboard that looked like a seashell. I painted it gray.

My friend was pleased and her little girl was also. The child liked the water effect. The room had the effect of living under the water. I used dark blue carpet and draperies.

I got the idea when my friend told me her little girl enjoyed Florida and enjoyed swimming.

An idea on the sea painted wall room if you leave out the swimming child painted on the wall. You could add a wooden board with my poem on it.

Selected Poems

If I Were A Fish

If I were a fish

I would explore the ocean floor

Up to the ocean top I'd soar

If I were a fish

I'd never blink or sink to the bottom

Of the ocean dish

If I were a fish

Bright orange and black would be my colors

If I had my druthers

If I were a fish

When I jump to the air

And turn in midair

To return to the ocean blue

The same as new

If I were a fish

I'd swim alongside the mighty wale

To the ocean's swirling whirls

If I were a fish

I'd hide behind a rock

So I wouldn't be the larger fish's meal

Then I'd steal away in a swish

If I were a fish

Also on the bed you might want to add pillows with

an orange and black fish on them, in other words, with some seashell cushions, and maybe

a seahorse pillow. You can draw the designs on paper and then use them as patterns. It's an

original idea for a child's room. It gives the effect of living in the water.

Congratulations C.E.O.

Congratulations on being elected C.E.O. of your company. It's time to fill your closets with silk blend suits. And on the back of your hand, there on your wrist, sport a Rolex watch. Take those narrow curves and keep your nerves in your new BMW car. Order some dress monogram socks; dye your locks. Wear only the best leather shoes. Always read the latest news. Be sure your dress shirt pockets are full of gold and silver pens. To be without them is a sin. Don't be without that platinum card. Walk like a king. Call the restaurant and make reservations. Take your honey and go out on the town. Dance like a clown.

South Coon Creek Our Summer Retreat

It's 85 degrees and there is river creek up to our knees. After we get in our boat we head to the big rock. There we'll throw out the anchor. Then we'll let down the Cokes for cooling.

We'll swim to the sandy beach and rest. There we'll swim and explore the underground cave.

After the picnic lunch
we'll fish.
In the water they're jumping.
When we real them in
in the boat they're thumping
South Coon Creek
Is our summer retreat.

The Hummingbird

The nosey little hummingbird, although he's small, he's a wonder. He hovers in midair. At him you stare. Turquoise and pink with a touch of yellow. His beak is sharp and long. After partaking of the nectar from the flowers. He flies in midair on his back, that I have discovered. He investigates all around up and down in a hover. He's seen in spring, summer, and autumn in the valley and the mountains. The humming bird is a beautiful bird. One to watch and observe.

My Grandbaby Sweet

Oh! my grandbaby you're so sweet,

it's such a pleasure seeing you in you little jumpie

    seat.

Why! you remind me of Little Bo Peep.

In your apron, dress, sitting with your little naked

    feet,

Your eyes are blue, your hair so blond of you I am so

    fond.

Melody your name is rhapsody.

You'll grow up soon and run and play, so enjoy your

    stay.

You're starting a journey, may God bless you my sweet,

sitting in your little jumpie seat with your little

    naked feet.

(My Grandbaby Is Three)

My grandbaby is three. She can walk, run, and have a lot of fun. Most any sunny day she can be found at play on the playground swinging big back and forth.

Fried chicken and French fries are her favorite foods. She likes fried shrimp when she's in the mood. She's a little bossy and always in her kids. She can hold her won with the day care kids.

A curly bob is her coiffure. She loves her nanny that's for sure. A party is her wish; she can dance the fish. If your going to the mall, I suggest you beckon her call. If you forget, she'll sit down and bawl!

Reflections In Time

There in the mirror, our reflection is.

A living soul awake.

A gift from God in time and space.

We, the human race.

In the mirror, on the ground,

On the water our reflection's found.

Many years, our reflections aboun.

We live our time in space

On this earthly place.

When it's time to sleep,

No more our reflections keep.

In the twinkling of an eye, we leap

Into a spirit world by the power alone.

We meet with the ones we love.

Spring

It's spring, the tulips are up. So are the buttercups. I feel like I want to sing. It's spring, the dogwoods are in bloom. There is a bud in pink and white. What a beautiful sight! The birds are singing. Pastels of flowers are all around the house. Azaleas are spread out the color of magenta. The grass is green. It's time for a fling! Don't you know it's spring? The birds sing. Soon the little Easter Bunny will be here. That's very clear. It'll be time to dye eggs again and hunt for them. The April showers will bring more flowers. It's life anew. I no more blue. It's spring, I want to sing!

Oh, Me, Oh, My! It's The Fourth Of July

Oh, me, oh, my! It's the Forth of July.

Mom's in the kitchen cooking some pie

Dad's on the back porch grilling on the grill

We'll eat hot dogs and burgers 'til we get our fill!

Hey, I see my cousin

We have them by the dozens.

We're in a good mood to enjoy some food.

We'll stay up through the night

To see the firecrackers in flight!

We'll stay and sit until the last show of light.

We'll all marvel at the show of sparkling light.

Oh, me, oh, my, it's a happy celebration

On the Fourth of July.

Autumn

It is autumn, a season filled

with warm days and cool nights.

The mountains are arranged with

hues of red, orange and yellow.

There is still time to sit in

our lawn chairs and enjoy

watching the squirrels scurry

across the lawn with a nut

in their clutches.

The sun warms us as we view a few

leaves scatter from their branches.

Long walks are pleasurable.

Big orange pumpkins are used for decoration.

It is autumn, a beautiful season

filled with warmth and beautiful hues.

One Day In September

One day in September we will always remember. We knew not the cause of the terrible twin falls. We are a God-fearing nation. In God we trust. We met in our churches to pray. In or land we want to stay.

The president met with our heads of state to make a plan to defend this land. Old Gory in flow to assure us at home. Together with the armed forces and the almighty power, we will resume the hour. We have sent out the fleet. We will not accept defeat. It's peace we seek.

October Day

As I sat on an old tree stump in the woods near our cabin -- I noticed a tree lay fallen on the ground. Lightning had struck it. It was split and dry. It made no sound -- my ear was not here when it hit the ground.

I heard an "eou-eou" sound. Then a bird -- the ground was full of leaves. Amber wet leaves. There was a mist in the air. I breathed in and out. I felt it was good to be alive.

Suddenly I heard a rustling through the bush. It was a deer. I stayed a while. It romped and stomped -- until our eyes met. Then it fled, fast it ran -- through the clearing.

I noticed it was getting late in the day -- I promised to have dinner ready when my family arrived home. While there was still enough light condescending down through the trees -- to light the pathway home. I must leave for I have a promise to keep. I have a promise to keep.

Christmas On Battery Hill

Just after dark the flow of cars start

Around the hill they go, it's a festive show!

Santa and his reindeer are on all the front lawns

Along with all the nativity scenes

On every door you will see wreaths

Wrapped in lights of white and topped with red velvet
  bows

On the mound you may find carolers singing *Silent Night*
  and *Joy to the World*

The snow coming down in a swirl

All around the hill during Christmas time

You can find cars driving around and down

Enjoying the festive sights

Of white lights and sounds

Winter's Cold Breeze

As I sit by my window, I can see the snow.

The winter's breeze takes the falling snow to the side of the trees. The children pout; they can't go out until the sun comes out. They put on their hooded coats in mid afternoon.

They run out and play the rest of the day! On snow-filled lawns they drop to the knees and gather snow for creme.

I'll stay by the fireside if you please

during winter's cold breeze.

I have sincerely enjoyed writing, OH, TO BE A DECORATOR.

From the author,

Janice W. Hughes

Janice Williams Hughes earned an associate degree in decorating after attending business college. Through ICS. She and her husband owned and operated a furniture business in Alabama. She grew up in a political family. Janice and her husband are grandparents, and still reside in Alabama.